C000195459

Greener b
the hill

very best wishes
from Edna Hunneysett
November 2017

Edna Hunneysett

chipmunkapublishing
the mental health publisher

Edna Hunneysett

Acknowledgements

My first attempt at writing this book began about 35 years ago. I'm very grateful to Keith Proud, a producer at the time at a BBC local radio station, who not only encouraged me to write but painstakingly typed my first manuscript from my long hand.

Around eighteen years ago, I redrafted the manuscript with new ideas and help from our youngest daughter, Elizabeth, to whom I am most grateful, for her time, patience and encouragement.

I thank Mary, my sister; and Christopher, one of our sons, both of whom read my latest redraft and recommended further minor improvements.

Lastly, but most importantly, I thank my husband for his continuous support and especially for his expertise and patience over many years helping me to overcome computer 'hiccups!'

Edna Hunneysett

Published by
Chipmunkapublishing
United Kingdom

http://www.chipmunkapublishing.com

Copyright © 2017

ISBN   Edna Hunneysett 2017

The grass is greener on the other side of the hill

Proverb

Other books by the author

Our Suicidal Teenagers: Where Are You God?
Pastoral Care Mental health
From The Heart: Mental health

Greener beyond the hill
is the author's first mystery novel

Edna Hunneysett was born in 1940 and spent her childhood on a remote farm on the Yorkshire moors. She attended a convent boarding grammar school following which, she worked for the Inland Revenue.
She married in 1961 and has eight children, grandchildren and great grandchildren.
From 1977 to 1991, she worked part-time at a BBC local radio station.
She gained a BA Hons (Div) in 1995 and an MA in 1998.
In 2014, Edna and her husband returned to the Yorkshire moors and live in a small village close to her roots.

Edna Hunneysett

Greener beyond the hill

1942

'At last,' thought Mary. 'Today is the day!' It was almost the end of October and the sale of Mr and Mrs Moorhouse's miscellaneous pieces of farming equipment, household goods and any remaining livestock was finally to take place as the elderly couple were retiring. Mary could hardly wait for them to leave. 'Then they will go and the house will be ours,' she thought, happily.

Mary stretched her arm across the mattress to see if Tom, her husband, was there. But just as she'd expected, he'd crept out much earlier to help Mr Moorhouse sort out lots in the farmyard for the sale. It had been her intention to stay with their children on the nearby farm of Tom's cousin Charlie, at his wife Dorothy's suggestion, until the Moorhouses left Bankside farm. Tom was very keen to move back North before the Moorhouses left because he wanted to be at the sale to join in the bidding if his slender means allowed, for anything he deemed essential for his future work on this rented farm.

A late letter from Dorothy scuppered Mary's plans. Dorothy's children were ill with whooping cough. As Mary did not want her children to be unnecessarily in contact with such a distressing ailment, her only alternative was a request to stay with the Moorhouses for a few days to which they kindly agreed. Tom would be with her in the evenings but he was to spend each day at Crossbeck farm helping Charlie. She had been dreading this beginning at Bankside farm and the Moorhouses' removal day seemed a long time in coming.
'But it's here,' thought Mary, brightening up at the thought. 'We can bring in our own few pieces of furniture from the outbuilding where we stored them when we came. It will just be us and our little ones.'

Mary and Tom arrived at Bankside farm in a removal van some days ago, with their three small children and in the back of the van, alongside their scant possessions, a small assortment of livestock. Mary remembered, ruefully, the reason why they have so little furniture. They sold the best of it to raise cash to put towards buying the horse and later a cow. Mary was very fond of their first married possessions chosen together and now they were gone.

Tom, her husband, explained that farm work could be done with borrowed implements but livestock needed to be bought, such as a horse to pull the plough, the chain harrows, the grass cutter and the like and a cow to provide milk and calves. Some of these words were strange to a town girl like Mary who knew nothing about farming. She felt sad to think of her personal possessions being replaced by animals but was looking forward to the future envisaging the pleasure of buying for their new home. When they finally decided to move back up North to a farm, from their small rented cottage, she imagined a large farmhouse kitchen with an oak dresser, oblong table and chairs, and plenty of storage cupboards. Mary allowed herself to indulge in these fanciful thoughts with no conception of the reality that lay ahead as her knowledge of farmhouse kitchens was virtually nil. Her dreams were shattered after discovering the reality of the situation over the last days.

'Never mind. I'll see Tom more often,' she thought, consoling herself. 'He'll be popping in and out during the day for frequent mugs of tea and five-minute chats in between the farm work instead of going off to work early and returning late.'

With these thoughts, Mary snuggled back under the covers for a few more minutes before embarking on the busy day ahead. Black curls lay over Mary's forehead and under her deep-set brown eyes overshadowed by thick black lashes, dark shadows were visible. She was almost twenty-seven years old, a normally slim and energetic young woman, but the last few years had taken their toll on her in coping with Emma, twenty-seven months, Martha aged three, and four-year old Tim.

In the early stages of pregnancy again, Mary felt very nauseous and listless. She closed her eyes and let her mind wander back to the halcyon days of courtship, being held in Tom's strong arms, dancing the hours away in the village halls around Whitby town. Her father, originally from the Scottish border country, was transferred to the small seaside town in Yorkshire in his work as an office clerk. He was happy to move with his younger daughter, leaving behind his elder one already in employment, as he was very unsettled since the death of his wife some years previously. Mary was a clever girl but, having reached her fourteenth birthday on moving, did not return to school. She found employment working in a sweet shop.

In time, her father took over a small local public house in one of
the villages on the outskirts of Whitby giving Mary further
employment helping behind the bar on weekend evenings which is
when Tom entered her life. She recalled her first memory of him,
tall and lean with dark straight hair combed back and so
handsome, she thought, as he walked into the pub with his mates.
His face was alight and his hazel-coloured eyes twinkled. The first
time he spoke to her, she felt her heart fluttering. She was
painfully shy and unsure how to deal with his obvious interest.
Each time in those early months whenever he appeared at the pub,
her heart turned over as she sensed him approaching the bar. Was
it deliberately planned that he seemed to frequent the pub when
she was on duty. She returned home romanticising her knight in
shining armour.

Mary stirred, feeling slightly more relaxed and content, after
reminiscing over this tall dark stranger whom she eventually
married. She knew he wanted to have his own farm one day. She
learnt that Tom, having left school at fourteen years of age
equipped only with his common sense and a good grounding in
farming, was determined to succeed and earn a living. He met
many country lasses but, once seeing Mary, was captivated by this
vivacious curly-haired brunette. He found her appealingly
curvaceous. The moment he set eyes on her pulling pints behind
the bar, he decided that she was the one for him. Tom oozed
charm, unlike Charlie, his cousin and drinking partner, who,
although the better dancer of the two, was a little dour. It was Tom
who caught the lasses when he had a mind to. Tom worshipped,
wooed and won his Mary. All of this delighted her.

Mary opened her eyes. She needed to drag herself out of the warm
blankets on the make-shift bed. Tom warned her that plenty of
folks would be turning up for the sale.
'It will be mugs of tea all round,' he said, jokingly. Mary hoped
not. They had scarcely any mugs or cups and Mrs Moorhouse's
pots and pans were already packed for their move out. She glanced
over to her children, still soundly sleeping. It was so early. Mary
was feeling nauseous again. It seemed to come in waves.
'When would this wretched sickness ease off?' she questioned
herself. She curled up a little longer, reliving their first encounter

with Mr and Mrs Moorhouse after that long journey, 'and what a journey that was,' she mused.

Whilst wondering what she had let herself in for, Mary began dozing. She floated back to the events that started with that letter she received from Dorothy, Charlie's wife. She met Charlie, Tom's cousin, when courting. Charlie was dark-haired, tall and lean like Tom but not quite so handsome, in Mary's opinion. He'd married a quiet, mousy-haired girl from a village near to his birthplace. Dorothy was a sensible choice, Tom's sister, Gertie, declared.

'She'll make a good hardworking farmer's wife, I reckon,' she said to Charlie, 'unlike our Tom's lass. What's she called? Mary, that's it.'

'Aye, I warned him,' responded Charlie, scowling somewhat with his beetle brows lowered. 'I told him that she'll be no good for a farmer's wife, a slip of a thing like that from town, and do you know what he retorted. *If I burns me backside, I'll sit on blisters.* He wouldn't be told.' Charlie grunted a note of pessimism. Tom's sister Gertie was equally unflattering in her judgment of Mary. 'That flighty bit from town,' was how she'd described her.

Gertie, dominant and forthright, broad and buxom, helped to raise Tom after their mother died whilst he was still at school. With their father's help, she'd become responsible for working the family's rented farm which was remotely situated in a valley alongside a tributary of the river Esk outside Shepton, a village on the Yorkshire moors. Over the years, she'd kept a motherly eye on her brother's activities, and,

'them from towns were no good for country folk,' she'd stated, adamantly. Tom followed his heart in defiance of these comments.

After they married, Mary and Tom left Tom's native Yorkshire to go South for work. Rose cottage was the accommodation offered along with his job. It was one of four terraced cottages situated up a small lane, near an outlying hamlet, some miles from Stratford-on-Avon. Mary imagined a quaint country cottage, with straggling ivy and bedecked with rosebushes, a little wicker gate and stone pathway leading to a rustic wooden door with a delicately-coloured and warm interior. Nothing could have been further from the truth. It was devastating having her fantasies blown away but she tried to see the positive and thought that maybe she could improve on the gloomy décor and somehow block out the draughts from the windows. Possibly, she could make a little pathway by cleaning the old broken stones covered in weeds and moss. Somehow, that never happened as babies quickly arrived on the scene and totally occupied her time.

Mary struggled over the years especially after the birth of Emma, with endless nappies to wash, many broken nights and tiring days. There were no relatives around to visit or ask help from. The only respite came when Betty arrived. The War Ministry was asking for lodgings for young women who were willing to work on farms replacing many of the labourers who signed up to join the Forces. This young lady arrived after Tom and Mary agreed they could take in one lodger by putting Tim in the tiny box room providing the land girl was happy to share Martha's bed in her small bedroom. Emma was feeding at night time and slept in her cot close by Mary and Tom.

Betty was a delight. A down-to-earth chubby girl with masses of ginger hair tied in a bushy ponytail, she was constantly singing the latest pop tune and was a massive help to Mary over the next few months when she wasn't working. Betty worked irregular hours but having never been on a farm or lived in the countryside, she found the whole experience an adventure and it was a sad day for the Holmes family when she moved on.

Betty was greatly missed especially by Mary whose spirits flagged after the land girl left. Night after night, Tom returned home to a very tired wife and chores waiting to be done as Mary found herself unable to cope. Gone were all her plans for renovating the cottage. Just surviving each day was a feat. Soon the dreaded stage of baby crawling became a reality. Emma was a source of constant anxiety to Mary. She explored the nooks and crannies in the cottage finding spiders curled up in corners, or mice droppings in the scullery. Woe betide if Mary left the door open as Emma immediately made a beeline for the open space, engineering herself over the step and heading off down the field. On one of these occasions, Tom, returning home earlier than usual, found her sitting among the grass. He was perturbed at finding Emma so far from the cottage but pushed it to the back of his mind, not wanting to criticise Mary and add to her distress.

It was the letter from Charlie and Dorothy that changed things. Charlie's affection for Tom, his cousin, was akin to a brother's. He knew Tom would love to come back to Yorkshire and that prospects would be better for him farming his own land than continuing working as a labourer. Charlie was keeping his ears to the ground regarding available, rented farmland. He persuaded his young wife to write periodically to Mary and Tom with any news, even though Dorothy struggled to make time for such an occupation because, as well as helping on the farm, she was preoccupied looking after their young children. They were renting a smallholding, Crossbeck farm, in the hamlet of Moorbeck on the Yorkshire moors and it kept them busy every minute of each day.

Moorbeck was situated in a small valley tucked away on the moors above Whitby with a tributary of the river Esk running through it. Although picturesque in summer, it was bleak and desolate in winter. It contained two smallholdings: Bankside farm, occupied by an elderly couple, the Moorhouses, due for retirement, and Charlie Holmes's place, Crossbeck farm, situated on the far side of the valley. Both properties were part of a large estate and all business was dealt with through an agent, employed by the owner. Once a year, all tenants were invited to a dinner and to pay their annual rents. At the last gathering, Charlie got wind of the Moorhouses' intentions to retire and put in a good word to the agent about Tom being a local lad, an excellent worker and was available and looking to rent his own farm. From that time, Mr Moorhouse regularly updated Charlie on the progress being made.

Around the time of Emma's second birthday, Charlie learnt that the Moorhouses had finally decided on a retirement date and that their rented farm, Bankside, run down and dilapidated, was up for re-rental. On Charlie's instructions, correspondence increased between Dorothy and Mary and Tom about the chances of Tom taking over Bankside farm.
'It seems a good idea,' Tom thought, thinking about a move to Bankside farm. He was sitting by the fire late one evening with Mary already in bed, tired out from her busy day with their three, lively offspring. He poked the fire to resurrect a flame from the dying embers and pulled his cigarettes from his jacket pocket. Taking a spill from the newly acquired spill holder on the

mantelpiece, he poked it in the flame and when lit, held it to his cigarette. He drew in deeply.

'Can't beat a good little woodbine,' he thought. Tom knew his present farm labourer's wage could not possibly achieve what he desired for their children. He wanted to work his own farm instead of labouring and always held the desire and hope of being back among his own solid Yorkshire mates. This seemed an ideal opportunity. Charlie would be nearby to give advice and share farm implements until such a time as Tom could afford his own, and Tom would only be a few miles from his dad's place. Tom sighed. He was tired. 'Makes sense to me,' he reasoned. 'I'll ask Missus in morning about it.' With that, he threw his tab end into the dying embers, swilled his face at the kitchen sink and paddled quietly upstairs to bed.

'What do you think, lass?' Tom questioned Mary over breakfast, drinking tea from his pint mug whilst Mary was struggling to put Emma into the old, worn and scratched, wooden high chair, about third-hand when they'd been given it. Emma persisted in scurrying to every corner of the room each time Mary made a grab at her. Martha and Tim were already seated on their chairs for their breakfast. Mary finally cornered her mischievous daughter, fastening the leather strap around Emma and the chair to make her secure, before replying.

'I'll talk later, Tom. I just can't listen with these three around. Have a chat with Mr Snaith. He'll understand your reasons and give you good advice.' Mr Snaith was Tom's boss, a robust and genial sort of fellow whom Mary always found to be pleasant and courteous.

'You don't mind us going then?'

'I think we ought to if it means more money for us.' Mary burst into tears. She was not feeling well.

'What's up, lass? Don't cry,' Tom said, soothingly, as he put his arm round his wife. She blinked back tears through her thick lashes. 'Don't you want to go?'

'It's not that. I guess we're having another one and… I don't know how we'll manage… if we stay here. If renting our own spot means more money, more space, then we'd better go,' she replied, with little sobs in between short breaths. Tom gave his wife a hug, kissing her on the cheek.

'Well, I guessed as much, the way you've been these last couple of days. Don't worry, lass. We'll manage fine. It will be a good move.'

After further reassuring words, Tom, taking his frayed working jacket from the nail behind the door, made his way out, leaving Mary smiling and more able to face the day. Tom went to work determined to discuss matters with his boss and see what advice he could offer. Following a chat and with words of encouragement from Colin Snaith, Tom set the wheels in motion for a move to Bankside farm, communicating through the agent with a letter, dictated by Tom and written by Mary. The good news arrived within days.

The information from Dorothy's latest letter was that the Moorhouses' farm sale of stock and machinery was imminent. Soon Mary was packing their belongings into boxes but found this to be something of a nightmare.

'No, Emma, no,' was her constant cry. Emma found packing pots, jugs, jars, and such like, fascinating and as soon as Mary turned her back, Emma was pulling at the paper and unravelling packages neatly stacked in readiness. One afternoon, amid all this activity, Emma made her way up the steep stairs, sat on the top step and waved her tiny hand to the horrified faces below.

'Isn't she clever, Mammy?' shouted Martha. Mary was unimpressed. She was already on edge as she tried to keep on top of the washing whilst struggling to pack clothes and belongings and yet keeping enough for the day's use.

'What are you eating, Emma?' she screamed, having dashed upstairs to rescue her daughter. She forced two fingers into Emma's clamped-up mouth and hooked out broken eggshell.

'Where have you got that from?' she questioned, not expecting an answer. Only yesterday, Emma upturned a bowl of eggs leaving some half broken with their contents spilt and others with small cracks in and leaking slightly. Others rolled around in the slimy mess like footballs on a muddy, wet field.

'Emma is naughty,' Martha said.

'Tim,' shrieked Mary, as she brought Emma down from her high perch, 'come and watch her and don't let her go up again.'

'Are we really going in a big van?' asked Tim, as he struggled with his little sister to deter her from climbing the stairs.

'Yes, but please, for now, be good and quiet and watch the girls whilst mammy packs,' pleaded Mary, wiping her furrowed brow with dirty fingers. Black print from the newspapers salvaged by Tom from his boss for use in packing, was staining her hands and now her face was streaked too. 'When will Tom come home?' she questioned herself, in desperation. 'Doesn't he know I can't manage all this on my own? Do the children really have all these toys?' It seemed to Mary to be an endless assortment of bricks, balls, dolls, teddies, tiny cars, books and crayons. They were mostly homemade or second hand. Tom roughly carved out toy pull-a-longs and Mary was a neat hand at sewing old material into teddies and dollies and stuffing them with even older material. Tim, Martha and Emma, now aged four, three and two, had no intention of parting with their treasures.

'I want,' started Martha, as she danced from one foot to the other and Mary could see that an urgent visit was needed across the yard to the earth closet. She dragged Martha by the hand across the cobbles and swung her through the cracked wooden door with its peeling paint. Down with her knickers and up onto the wooden board and just in time. She clung to Mary's hands as the seat was high from the ground for a little lass. 'Done, Mammy,' she gleefully shouted, proud that she had promoted herself from the potty to the big seat. Everything accomplished, they made their way back to the kitchen to be met with cries from Emma. Two little arms stretched up to Mary with a face running with tears turned upwards.
'Whatever's the matter darling?' cooed Mary, hugging to herself a sobbing Emma. 'Tim,' Mary shouted. 'Tim, what did you do?' Tim hung his head.
'It was a game but Emma can't push as hard as me.'

'Will it never end?' thought Mary. 'Does it never stop? Always noise and chatter, shouts and tears.' To her relief, Tom strode in through the open door. She fell into his arms but barely had she started her tale of woe when they heard screams from Emma. Tim decided to pretend his baby sister was a great, moving toy and having grabbed her tiny feet to delay her creeping, was sitting on her back gleefully shouting,
'Gee-up, gee-up, gee-up.' Martha, meanwhile, was giving encouraging swipes at Emma's rear end.

'Tim, get off. You're too heavy for her,' shouted Tom, angrily, taking a swipe at Tim, but missing as Tim immediately dismounted with great speed. Rescue came in the form of two strong hands that whisked Emma up into the air. She clung to her daddy. Her tears subsided and tranquility once more descended on the Holmes family, but for how long?

That night, Mary lay in bed, worrying. She was so weary but could not sleep. She tossed and turned. She was originally unconcerned about moving but now she was anxious.
'What would the journey to Yorkshire be like?' she wondered. 'Would they manage when they got there?' Tom would be working long hours, she knew that. 'Would she make a good farmer's wife? Would it be very lonely with no neighbours next door?' Eventually, Mary drifted into an uneasy sleep.

Mary awakened early the next morning, after a very restless night, to finish packing and make sandwiches to take with them. Whilst Tom was carrying boxes outside, four-year old Tim was watching through the kitchen window for the van with great anticipation.
'It's here. It's here,' he shouted, gleefully.
'Martha, stay near me,' yelled Mary to their three-year old. She carried Emma out and approached the van. There was wild excitement among the two older children as the removal van pulled up and they ran through the open door to watch the goings-on.
'I'll need a hand with loading up,' the van driver explained as Tom went to meet him. 'Sometimes I have a mate with me but he's off sick. Sorry an' all but didn't want to let you down,' he said, gruffly, wiping his nose on his sleeve. Thick-set and short, he looked burly enough to lift a few boxes and bits of furniture.
'Okay,' replied Tom. 'There isn't that much. We'll manage between us. More room for us in cab, anyway,' he added, before going back into the cottage.
'Keep out of the way while the boxes are loaded,' called Mary to her children, but to no avail. They ran around and tried to climb into the back of the van. It was very exciting for them.

Mr Snaith promised Tom a leaving present. He pulled up in his truck, heaving his large, stocky frame out of the vehicle and called over the van driver.

'You don't mean that's coming?' the driver asked in amazement as Mr Snaith began tugging a crate out of his truck.
'I certainly do.' The crate contained a huge, saddleback pig that was snorting and snuffling in its confined space.
'Ugh,' said Tim, gazing at it. 'It smells.'
'Good healthy smell, that,' chortled Mr Snaith. The crate was loaded into the van and pushed up alongside a wardrobe. It was a wonderful gesture from an appreciative boss who found Tom to be a reliable and conscientious worker.

'Come over here, lad,' Mr Snaith called to Tim. 'These are for you, something for you to look after.' He showed Tim two rabbits, one black and one white, cowering in a small hutch. 'Pet rabbits, they are,' explained Mr Snaith. A smile slowly spread across Tim's face.
'Thank you,' he said, in his most grown-up manner. 'Thank you so much.' Tim called to Mary as she came out of the cottage. 'Look, Mammy, they're mine, they're mine,' he shouted, joyously. Mr Snaith turned to Mary.
'Mrs Tom, I've got something for you, too. Bantam chicks. Smashing little eggs, you'll get off these for the children, and I wish you well up there,' he added, cordially. Mary, overcome with shyness, smiled her thanks as she reached out to take the box of chicks from Mr Snaith. She'd never heard of bantams.
'I must ask Tom, later,' she thought. Colin Snaith placed the rabbit hutch inside the van alongside some boxes and Mary handed him back the chicks to put inside also.
'Drummer should be at Charlie's farm when you arrive, Tom,' Colin Snaith added, as Tom appeared, carrying a box over to the van.
'What's Drummer, Daddy?' questioned Tim, inquisitively.
'It's a horse, son.'
'You mean we'll have our very own horse, Daddy, and a pig as well and my rabbits and mammy's bantams,' he exclaimed, quite amazed at such possessions.
'Aye, lad, and we'll have more than that, I hope.'

Mary, with Emma in her arms, took one last look at the cottage, upstairs and down to make sure nothing was left behind. She stood Emma on the floor and took her hand whilst picking up a large bag of necessities packed earlier for the journey. After making sure that Tim and Martha were outside by the van, she turned the key in the lock of the cottage door for the last time and placed it under a large, flat stone. Milly, from next door, called in earlier to say her goodbyes and promised Mary that she would give the cottage a quick once-over and return the key to the landlord.

Mary felt a little sad but also with hope and expectation of better times to come. She gave a helping push to Tim climbing into the cab and likewise with Martha before squeezing past them in the cab, and settling herself in with Emma on her knee and her bag at her feet. She twisted her legs around the side of it to achieve a little more comfort. Tom clambered up and nestled in beside Mary. They somehow managed to squeeze Tim between them, Martha being nursed by Tom.

'I'm squashed,' Tim moaned, after Tom slammed the door. Tim felt very hemmed in.

'I really can't move any further,' stated Mary, anticipating a wearisome journey.

'All in?' asked the driver, looking at his crowded cab.

'Aye,' replied Tom. The driver climbed into the van and slammed the door. He started the engine and set off leaving Mr Snaith waving until they were out of sight. Mary turned to Tom and smiled. A whole new life was about to begin.

The feelings of joyful anticipation and peace were short lived with Mary vividly remembering what a trial it was trying to keep the little ones occupied on the journey North. They were barely able to see out of the cab window due to mist and light rain and soon became bored. Books, pencils and paper helped. It was only a short time later that Emma began wriggling and squirming inside the cab.

'I want to get out. I want to get out,' she pleaded. 'Let me down. I don't like it in here. Don't like that noise.' The squeaking, squealing, squawking and grunting of their livestock in the back, was upsetting her. She found sitting on Mary's knee very tedious. The windscreen wipers, moving to and fro, on this damp, drizzly day in October, fascinated her for a while but now she was bored and restless. 'Let me go, Mammy, let me go,' she demanded.

Martha was a fidget, squirming and twisting on Tom's knee.

'Not again,' the driver muttered, as Mary asked for another stop, in response to a request from Tim.

'Tim, just stand at the side of the van out of sight,' Mary whispered. 'There's nowhere else here you can go.' Thirty minutes later, another stop. 'Can't you wait, Martha?' No, she couldn't. 'It is less dignified for a little girl,' thought Mary, as Martha squatted by the side of the van. Tim kept up an incessant run of questions to Tom about the new home.

'Will we have lots of cows, Daddy? Where will they sleep? What do they eat? What shall I give my rabbits?'

'Daddy, Tim's got his elbow sticking into me,' wailed Martha.

The van driver, a dour-faced individual, showed his displeasure with his sighs and grumbling. He was not happy with the over-crowded cab and inevitable frequent stops when one of the children needed to get out. He was not fond of little ones and found these three, very noisy and irksome. Visibility was poor. This added to his frustrations. The slight drizzle turned into heavy rain lashing the windows, slowing him down.

'Keep a lookout for a Whitby sign,' he yelled to Tom, above the noise of the engine and clamour of the children. Half an hour later, the driver swung the van onto the moor road above Whitby.

'Nearly there now,' shouted Tom, half-turning his head to Mary. 'Thank God for that,' she thought. She shifted uncomfortably on the hard seat. The journey seemed so long. She felt hungry and sickly and coping with a wriggling child had not been helpful, but thankfully, Emma was now asleep. Martha, tired, because she had fallen asleep so late the previous evening due to excitement, was dozing on Tom's knee. Tim occupied himself with a picture book, having exhausted his supply of questions. Tom peered out through the rain-splattered window to study road signs and the countryside. They passed by familiar ones that pointed to the small villages he knew so well. A little past the sign to Windrush village, he noticed a cart track to the left.

'There,' he shouted, recognising the area as described by Dorothy in her last letter.

Even Mary was nodding off, using Tom for a head rest and with Emma snuggled into her and for a moment, as she came to, was wondering where she was. The van! Moving! The van screeched to a halt and reversed to where Tom was indicating.

'You expect me to drive down that?' the driver asked, irritatingly.

'Aye, there's no other way.' Cursing under his breath, the driver slowly turned on to the track, rutted with clods of earth and stones, running through the heather. Eventually, he drew up at a gate denoting the boundary of a farm on the way to Moorbeck. 'I guess this is Marsh farm,' Tom thought, recalling Dorothy's last letter. Tom climbed down to open the gate, disturbing Martha. 'Just sit there while I open gate,' he said to her. She frowned deeply at him and continued sucking her thumb.

'Never forget, lass,' Tom instructed Mary, on climbing back into the van, 'you always leave gates as you find them. Leave them shut if shut and open if open.' Mary nodded ascent. They continued along the track passing Marsh farmhouse and meeting up with another gate at the other end of the fenced-off land. Beyond was open moorland.

'Good grief,' exclaimed the driver. 'More moor? Where are we going?'

'Not far now,' reassured Tom, recalling Dorothy's detailed descriptions. 'We'll dip shortly as we go down in valley.' He surmised that this rough land was part of Bankside farm. The next gate opened on to fields and once through it, the track dropped sharply.

Mary peered out through the gloom to try to see what lay ahead as they nosed down the track. She made out the outlines of farm buildings to the left at the bottom of the bank, but little else as the rain and mist blocked any further viewing. She was nervous and full of trepidation that had increased as the journey progressed. Tim was terrified as the van was making its way slowly down the steep incline, and wondered if they would make it. His face was ashen and his fists were tightly clenched although no sound came from his lips. Very, very slowly, the van ground to a halt at another closed gate. Tim, along with his dad, joyously clambered out into the drizzle and after watching his dad undo the binder twine fastener, helped him drag the gate open for the driver to go through. Tom waved the driver on to the left.

The driver swung the wheel and the van crawled along the edge of the buildings to the farmhouse. They'd finally arrived. The van shuddered to a halt and the engine petered out but the snorting pig and cheeping chicks kept making their presence known. Tom, holding his son's hand, caught up, opened the cab door, and letting go of Tim, lifted Martha down and whilst still clasping Martha's little fingers, took Emma from her mother's arms as Mary lowered herself on to the cobbles. The rain was easing off as they walked carefully towards the farmhouse door picking their way over the rough stones.

A tall, thin, tired-looking woman with greyish-white hair, pulled well back and tied up with, what seemed to Mary, a piece of white bandage, appeared at the door. The man, standing behind her was big, broad, with a red, weather-beaten face and a grey moustache. 'You got here, then?' the bloke greeted Tom. 'I'm Ted Moorhouse and this is Missus. There's a pot of tea and a bite to eat on table. Come on in.' They trooped inside. Tom carried Martha, and Mary held Emma, with Tim right behind her. The removal man trailed behind.

Mary glanced around, realising that this was certainly not her dream kitchen. She was aghast as she took in some details. The walls were of uneven grey stone. A dirty bucket half full of slops of tea leaves, potato peelings and other left-overs was next to a woodworm-holed, small wooden table. Cobwebs and dead flies blurred the window pane, itself looking grey and murky. Hanging on the back of the door were dilapidated, heavy coats and jackets and nearby, pairs of wellington boots, caked in mud and grime around the bottoms. Buckets hung from long nails hammered into the far wall alongside a tin bath. An old, chipped, earthenware sink stuck out along an uneven stone wall next to a door opposite to the one they entered.
'That's door through t' buildings at back,' volunteered Mr Moorhouse, 'and that's copper,' he continued, pointing to a square-like, brick construction in the corner, 'for washing clothes.' Mary could see that it had a large scooped-out hollow and a tiny door at the bottom.
'For a fire to heat the water,' she thought. 'It must be.'
'We call this room, wash house,' Mr Moorhouse continued.

They went along a short stone-floored passage. He tapped on the door at his right.
'Coal house,' and with a tap on the left-hand side door, stated, 'dairy.' He opened a second door on his right and they walked into another room. 'Kitchen.' A fire crackled and flared at the far end of the room and the square table in the centre was laden with

sandwiches and cakes. It was a wonderfully appetising sight to the tired travellers. Mary washed six little grubby hands and three faces from a bowl of water on the sideboard along a right-hand wall. Mrs Moorhouse handed her a well-worn piece of towelling with which to dry them. There weren't enough seats but the adults mostly stood around and ate to their fill, the warmth from the fire creeping into their chilled bodies. Mary was offered a seat and nursed Emma who was unhappy at being woken up and disinclined to eat at first, but hunger overtook her and she joined in with the rest of them. Mugs of tea and cups of milk were gratefully accepted.

Hours later, after the men unloaded the Holmes's furniture into an empty outbuilding to be transferred to the farmhouse when the Moorhouses moved out, Mary and Tom were snuggled close in the back bedroom on a makeshift mattress. The rabbits were in their hutch in the garden whilst the bantams were free to roam in the hen house at the back of the farm buildings and the pig was in an empty sty. The children, sharing the bedroom, were asleep on the bed nearby, dreaming, no doubt, of bumpy roads, endless stops and a snorting pig.

Each parent was lying there in the darkness with many a thought flying around restless minds. Mary was weary and feeling despondent. It wasn't how she'd been anticipating and she was wondering if she could manage in this isolated place. Her thoughts were negative.
'Will Tom be able to make a living? How will I shop? Can I, a town girl, born and bred, come to terms with this old farmhouse, the animals and farm work and look after another tiny baby and the children?' In her over-tired and anxious state, she was unable to prevent tears rolling slowly down her face and she cuddled up closer to Tom. Tom was churning things over too. This farm was to him a necessity and a challenge.
'How else would his family survive if he did not provide?' he asked himself. 'I'll labour and sweat from dawn 'til dusk if I have to,' he thought. He was full of ambitions and his devotion was strong. He gently wiped the tears from Mary's cheeks with a piece of rag that substituted for a handkerchief and made a silent prayer for strength to look after her and their children. Eventually sleep overtook them and nothing further was heard except the breathing of five tired occupants, in this, their first night in their new home.

Greener beyond the hill

At an early hour, next morning, Tom crept out of bed to go to Crossbeck farm to help Charlie with the milking. Mary awoke a little later, stiff and nauseous. On arriving downstairs to get a cup of tea, Mary found Mrs Moorhouse setting the table for breakfast. Mary needed to visit the lavatory which was outside the house. She discovered it to be very small and draughty, with no lock on the door and the inside consisting of nothing more than a bucket boxed in and covered by a piece of wood with a hole in its centre, and some torn pieces of newspaper.

'Nothing new there then,' she thought. It was another cold, wet morning and she was feeling depressed. It didn't seem like her own home with Mrs Moorhouse around. Mary felt in the way. 'I can hear the children,' she said, despondently, when she came back in. 'I'll go and bring them down.'

Mary spent the following days living in the sitting room with her three little ones. She managed as best she could whilst they waited for the Moorhouses to sell up and move out. Tom made his way over to Charlie's every day helping on his farm. Not wanting to upset Mrs Moorhouse, Mary tried to keep her restless children in the sitting room but she needed to cook in the kitchen and wash clothes in the wash house on days when Mrs Moorhouse was not using the copper boiler. She found the days stressful and tiring. Tim and Martha were eager to explore outside, an added worry for Mary. There were many dangerous places on the farm that the children were not used to and Mary was constantly checking on the children when they all ventured out to explore a little. Sometimes Tim tagged along with his daddy and played at Crossbeck farm, coming back with glowing reports of the animals and what they did.

'I've seen Drummer,' he stated one day. 'He's a great big horse, this big,' he demonstrated, stretching his arms out wide. Drummer was being housed by Charlie until the Moorhouses moved out.

'Mary. Mary,' the voice was calling. It was Tom shouting from downstairs. Mary jolted. She opened her eyes. She tried to clear her thoughts as the chatter of her children was penetrating her tired, fuddled mind.

'Come on, Mammy,' chorused her children. 'Daddy's wanting you.' The sale! Mary remembered. It was today!

These sales attract a great many farmers from around the area, some of the farmers being eager to buy and others to enjoy the social occasion. In preparation for his move, Mr Moorhouse, over the weeks, had slowly been selling much of his livestock and some larger pieces of farming equipment. Over the last couple of days, Tom had helped Mr Moorhouse put the remaining miscellaneous tools and goods in piles in the stack yard ready for the auctioneer to sell to the highest bidder. This morning they were up very early stacking any unwanted furniture, crockery and kitchen utensils into heaps. Farmers drifted into the stack yard, having a last look at what was on offer before the auctioneer appeared with his clip board, ready to begin the sale.

Gertie, Tom's sister, put in a surprise visit. Gertie was curious to see how Mary was faring. She made her way into the farmhouse kitchen which was shambolic with pots and pans, cutlery etc. in boxes, some belonging to the Moorhouses and some that Mary had carried in from the outside building. Mary eyed her up and down. Gertie was wearing her boots with her overalls tucked inside, her round face, scrubbed and weather-beaten and with her straggly hair hanging out of a cap perched on her head.
'Come to help,' she volunteered.
'Well,' replied Mary, rather taken aback by this woman and feeling a little flustered. 'There's more stuff of ours in an outbuilding if you want to carry it in, please. Tom is outside and he'll show you which building. These aren't ours,' she said, pointing to the pile belong to the Moorhouses. 'You can stack them outside for the removal van, if you like. That would help, too.' Gertie set to, thinking that her own words were coming true, that this town lass was a bit out of her depth.

Another surprise. Tom's uncle Sam appeared. He was quite the gentleman. He biked the twenty miles or so from Middlesbrough and needed a drink before joining the farmers outside. He was of medium height, with a round face and odd wisps of grey hair remaining on his almost bald head. Uncle Sam was a great talker and very fond of his nephew. Mary greeted him warmly as she knew that her husband held his uncle in great affection. Although Gertie had cared for Tom since their mother's death, it was his mother's brother Sam, to whom Tom turned when needing advice. Tom walked in, having spotted his uncle come up the cobbles.

They were delighted to see each other. Gertie strode into the kitchen, her arms loaded with boxes.

'Dad says he hopes it all goes okay today and come and see him soon,' she said to her brother. 'He says to bring Mary and bairns with you. He's not up to much travelling these days. His arthritis is getting worse.' She nodded to her uncle and placed the boxes down before disappearing out again. Tom followed.

'See you later, Uncle,' he said, on leaving.

There was a lot of bantering among the farmers whilst the selling of livestock and farm machinery was taking place. The auctioneer moved from lot to lot with the interested farmers making their bids at each stop. As they moved around, Charlie introduced Tom to local farmers. Tom was acquainted with some of them from his pre-marriage days. A farmer Tom talked to, at length, was Nick Edwards from Windrush village, a friend from his earlier years. Nick was tall like Tom but broader, heavier built, with a weather-worn round face, fair hair and sporting a neatly trimmed moustache to match. He kindly offered Tom a horse called Daisy. 'She's a bit lame and not very good for work,' he explained, 'but she'll do okay as a team-mate for Drummer and make an excellent breeding mare.' Tom was delighted. Nick invited Tom to join him for a pint at Hunters Lodge public house in Windrush, after church, the following Sunday. This was customary in the village, he explained to Tom. Many Catholics went there for a pint after Mass. It was a chance for a catch-up on the latest stock prices or weather conditions, a topic never far from a farmer's mind, or even for a short game of dominoes before home for dinner. It was a highlight in their week.

'Now then Henry, meet your new neighbour, Tom,' Nick voiced, as he turned to another young man skirting the crowds. Henry was the youngest of four children at Marsh farm. He was a quiet, retiring lad, in his late teens, stocky in build with a shock of unruly ginger hair, and wearing glasses as he struggled with a squint in one eye. He grinned at Tom before wandering off to inspect the lots in the hope that he might find something for his mam. Mrs Williams was getting on in years but a hardworking woman who brought up her four children on her own after the early death of her husband. Henry was very close to his mam. 'If you ever want a hand, Tom, young Henry is a great worker and always keen to earn a bob or two,' Nick offered.

Tom spied Mary wandering about with Emma and Martha as she was curious to see what happened at a farm sale. Tim had been out earlier enjoying trailing his dad around the stack yard. Tom made way to meet Mary and introduced her to Nick along with the girls who were the centre of attention for a short while. Nick explained that sadly he did not have children of his own but he was fond of children and took a great interest in his brother Ben's brood of five lads.

'You might see them around when you come for a drink. Our Ben is the landlord of Hunters.'

Another farmer making a point of introducing himself to Tom and Mary, was Jack Netherfield, who explained that he was a relatively new neighbour from one of the farms adjoining Bankside. Jack was tall, lean, fair-haired and good-looking. He was almost overconfident, leaning very close when he spoke. Tom felt uneasy when talking with him and was glad to move on to others. Mary lingered, quite enjoying a chat with this very amiable farmer. 'I must call in sometime seeing as I'm your neighbour,' was his parting quip whilst giving Mary a friendly smile and patting Martha on the head as he sauntered off to join in the bidding. Mary watched him disappear into the crowd and felt uplifted at meeting him and glad to know that he lived not too far away.

The sale was a good one with items being sold rapidly. One by one, the farmers dispersed after making their arrangements with Tom as to when they would remove their purchases if they weren't taking them on the day. Mary was relieved when the hustle and bustle died down. She was feeling a little less depressed, apart from the morning sickness and lethargy, knowing that soon they would be on their own again. Mary, never having lived on a farm, could not envisage the weeks and months that lay ahead without the regular weekly income she was used to and with hours of hard work and little reward.

'Tarra, Tarra,' the Moorhouse couple called as they walked out of Bankside farm for the last time, delighted with the very successful events of the last few hours. They were anxious to be off with the sale completed, telling Tom that if any items worthwhile were unsold, he and Charlie were welcome to have them.

'Bye,' shouted Mary. The children waved furiously, little Emma giving a serious queen-like wave as she clung to her mother's skirt. A great feeling of jubilation swept over Tom as he lifted his wife high in the air and swung her round the kitchen.

'Me, too. Me, too,' cried Martha. Smiling broadly, Tom whisked her up in the air and followed with Tim and Emma. Mary wiped the tears of joy from her eyes and joined in with hugs and kisses as waves of happiness swept over her. The sheep dog, Trigger, given to Tom by Charlie, wandered in and eyed this hilarious group with some surprise but after a quiet word from his master, he turned tail to walk back out to wait on the doorstep. Mary did not want animals in her kitchen. She made it plain from the start that the dogs would stay outside where, in her opinion, animals belonged. She glanced at Trigger and relented this time.

'It's all right, Trigger,' she called. 'Come in.' Trigger padded silently back and lay at his master's feet as Tom drunk a mug of tea.

What little furniture they possessed had been brought into the farmhouse with the help of Charlie and uncle Sam, before Charlie left for Crossbeck farm and uncle Sam, home to Middlesbrough. Boxes were in small piles on the cement floor, some half empty, but with more unpacking still to be done. Mary had yet to separate the boxes containing their gas masks, which everyone was given in case of a gas bomb attack.

'But thankfully, she's left me the blackout curtains,' thought Mary, very relieved, as she knew that windows must be covered at night to prevent a glimmer of light.

'Grand, that, lass, but I'll have to be away,' said Tom, placing his empty mug on the small, scuffed table. I've work to do. I'll see you later.' Giving his wife a hug, he pulled on his flat cap over his dark hair and strolled out in his size eleven boots with Trigger at his heels.

Much later that evening, each with a cup of tea and a woodbine and enjoying the last of the heat from the dying embers, Mary and Tom discussed the events of the day.

'Some nice folks,' Mary said. 'Charming man, that Netherfield fellow, who introduced himself to us. A neighbour too. That's good to know.'

'Well,' said Tom, 'I may be wrong but I just have a feeling there was something odd about him even though he was pleasant enough. I just didn't feel I could trust him and I don't know why. Grand meeting up with Nick though and getting another horse.'

With that, they went to bed but Mary couldn't settle to sleep. She lay awake churning over events since leaving their little cottage. Tom nudged her, breaking her chain of thought and bringing her back to the present.

'Settle down, lass,' he mumbled. 'It's over now. It's just us. Go to sleep.' But Mary struggled.

'Was this the beginning of an idyllic family life on a farm that she hoped for?' she questioned, very unsure of what the future might have in store, here at Bankside farm.

Greener beyond the hill

1943 Winter Spring

The following months were not as Tom would have liked or expected, especially concerning Mary. She found this new life almost unbearable. She hated it. She cried often and pleaded daily with Tom to take her away. It was a hard life and not at all as she had anticipated. Tom was never in to help her, but only for meals and mugs of tea. The children were constantly getting filthy in the mud and water that seemed to abound around the buildings. It was a cold winter with little money and few comforts. Apart from when at church on Sundays, Mary rarely saw anyone to talk to and she was lonely.

Early every morning, reaching out of bed to find the matchbox on the floor to light a candle, Mary struggled, dragging her weary body from the warmth of the bedding. Creeping downstairs, after quickly putting on her clothes and wrapping up with her old, thick, woolly grey cardigan, she lit the oil lamp before cleaning out the grate and lighting the fire with twigs from in the sack, collected by Tom the previous day. They did not ignite very quickly and the fire was only a glimmer for a while before slowly catching on. The lamp sent out an eerie glow from the centre of the table. As Mary carried it out to the wash house to fill the kettle from the water tap, she saw shadows moving in the corners. She heard squeaks and scurrying as the tiny mice that ventured out at night, scampered back into their homes.

'We must have some mousetraps,' she pleaded with Tom when he arrived downstairs, 'and that old cat, the one Moorhouses left, is useless. I can't stand mice droppings all over. Their feet marks are in the frying pan today because I forgot to put it away in the pantry last night. They'll find their way in there next. Then what will I do?'
'Aye, lass. Aye,' mumbled Tom, making a mental note to do something about it this time.
'But you must do something about it. You must. You always say *aye* but nothing gets done,' insisted Mary.
'Calm down, lass,' pleaded Tom, aware that Mary was getting hysterical over a few mice. 'Charlie's kittens are ready for weaning. I'll get one of them today. Tomorrow I'm off to Whitby. I'll get some traps.'

Tom pulled on his boots. He put on his torn jacket, and fastening it round his waist with a piece of string, strode out, pulling on his milking cap as he went. Tom was distraught. All winter, Mary struggled with mornings like this, with fires that would barely burn and mice that freely ran around. Tom knew it was tough but being heavily in debt to relatives and friends, having borrowed to buy stock and winter fodder, he knew there was no turning back. He must make a go of things. All through winter, he promised Mary that it would only be for six months. By doing this, he fervently hoped and prayed that, come spring, Mary would be adjusting to conditions at Bankside farm and that the warmer weather would bring out the beauty of Moorbeck and the happier side of farming life. This did not seem to be happening. By early spring, heavily pregnant, Mary was weary and depressed.

Tom tackled his new life with much determination but was experiencing a lot of frustration. It was not just milking cows by hand, working the land and doing repairs that kept him busy but other unexpected jobs kept cropping up. For instance, transporting the coal. Tom found out on one of his visits to Whitby for the weekly shopping that the coal wagons did not come into Moorbeck. All goods were left at the end of the track where it joined the tarmac road.
'Even coal?' he questioned. 'Bloody hell. Do you realise what that means?' he said, in exasperation. He had no choice but to shovel the loose coal onto the cart and bring it down to the farm. He made many journeys with Drummer and the cart, a two wheeled, two-sided vehicle with a hooked up back that let down to discharge its load. In this cart, Tom took the milk churn each day to the milk stand at the end of the cart track for the milk lorry to pick up and he collected an empty churn in exchange, ready for the next day's milk. In time, he arranged to alternate weekly with Charlie, each taking both lots of milk and picking up the empty churns.

When going into Windrush village, Tom found it quicker to turn right at the top of the bank out of Moorbeck instead of following the original track to the left passing Marsh farm. He cut across some moorland and went down through a deep hollow known as the Mudhole where the farm boundary was marked by the fence running around the outskirts of Tom's land. A gate in the fence in the hollow opened onto a flat stretch of track running by a beck, and the track continued uphill and onto more moorland eventually joining the tarmac road. The road to Windrush was directly opposite.

However, alongside the tough conditions, Tom found great comfort in his children. Tim spent many hours with his dad, chattering about the animals and asking questions. The girls greeted him with their laughing eyes and lifted his worries for a moment when he called in home. Emma and Martha adapted to their new life without much difficulty. They loved to see their dad coming in and out, giving them a word and a smile. He only had to sit down in his armchair for a moment before two dark-haired lasses climbed up, one on each knee for Tom to joggle up and down, their squeals of delight ringing through the air. They loved it.

Sometimes the girls clambered onto Mary's knee as she rested in her rocking chair, gently lilting to and fro. She gave her daughters many a cuddle while she sang lullabies and nursery rhymes, her sweet, soprano voice filling the air with music. These were happier moments in Mary's dark days. Something said to her outside church, one Sunday morning, by Mrs Williams, the elderly, greying-haired lady, with weather-beaten skin and kindly blue eyes, whom Mary knew lived at Marsh farm, went through Mary's mind repeatedly.
'You'll get used to it like an old moor ewe.'
'Will I?' Mary pondered. 'Will I really come to enjoy living here with our odd bits of second-hand furniture and few comforts, and with the long walk through the Mudhole and down to Windrush village for any sign of civilisation? Perhaps I will,' she thought, feeling her baby moving restlessly inside her. A feeling of warm contentment crept through her body. 'Time to get a move on,' she said. 'Down you go. Mammy must clean the shoes for church tomorrow.' The girls scampered off.

Next morning, they were eagerly waiting for Tom to come in from his work.
'Hurry up, Daddy. Hurry up, Daddy,' shouted Martha. It was Easter Sunday and they were all going to church. Drummer, with the cart, was standing patiently by the cobbles at the coals door. The door was so called because of the stack of coals that Tom

piled up around the side of the farmhouse near the front. They'd named the door in the wash house that led out to the buildings at the back of the house, the pigs door, as it opened opposite the pigsty. Tom was coming in through the pigs door, having washed his boots in the trough to remove all farm muck, leaving them clean and shining for his trip to church. It was quite a regular occurrence for Tom, Mary and the children to go to church when they could make it, but lately, Mary was mostly too tired to go and Tom took only Tim with him on Drummer. With today being Easter Sunday and her baby due in a few weeks, Mary wanted to go to Mass. The family made themselves as comfortable as possible in the cart, sitting on old, clean, empty hessian sacks. With a gee-up to Drummer from Tom, they set off.

'I'll do the gates, Daddy,' Tim called out as they approached the first one.
'Whoa,' shouted Tom, pulling Drummer to a halt to let Tim climb over the cart side and jump to the ground. Tim unhooked the string from the post and dragged the gate open. He closed it after them and pulled himself back up into the cart, landing in a heap among the girls and empty sacks. Bumpety-bump trundled the cart over stones and dips, the children lurching from side to side. They clung to Mary who was herself hanging onto a side of the cart with one hand whilst trying to support Emma with the other. As the horse pulled away from the Mudhole, the children slid down to the bottom of the cart, and with shouts and giggles, crawled back up to Mary.

Once they reached the end of the track, the journey was less rough as Drummer clip-clopped his way down the tarmac road to Windrush. Curiosity overcame the children and they knelt up to lean over the cart sides to wave at any cars that sped passed them. There were a few walkers about who happily returned their waves as the family passed by hedges, fields and lane ends. Eventually the horse and cart wound its way down Beggars bank into Windrush village. Tom pulled Drummer to the right and turned up the side of Hunters Lodge, to leave his horse in the stables at the back.
'Down you all come,' he said, swinging Emma and Martha to the ground, and giving a helping hand to Mary. Tim jumped but misjudged the distance and ended up with a bleeding knee from the rough stones.

'Oh dear,' sighed Mary. 'Let's tie a hanky around it. It should soon stop bleeding.'
'Off you go. I'll catch you up,' shouted Tom, as he led Drummer away to tie him up, having seen that Tim was no worse for his fall. Acknowledging his words with a smile, Mary took a little hand in each of hers and set off down the road to the church.

They customarily sat together in a bench near to the front of the church to the left of the aisle that ran from the doors at the back. Father Burnett, in his long robes, was standing in the pulpit, solemnly preaching, his loud and clear voice reaching all corners of this very old church with its colourful stained-glass windows and in need of a coat of paint.

'We're late again,' thought Mary, highly embarrassed at walking down the aisle of the crowded church with her little tribe whilst everyone else was sitting quietly. The priest paused and waited for them to settle in the bench. Mary took Emma onto her knee and with a child at either side to prevent squabbling, raised her eyes to the priest who smiled gently and continued with his sermon. Emma was fidgety during Mass. She could not see God and she could not understand what anyone was saying. She watched the flickering candles and saw what she thought was smoke coming out of a swinging object, but it had a very peculiar smell. She was nudged to kneel by Mary, and dragged to her feet at intervals to stand. She was told to *shush* if she dared to speak to Martha. Emma knew her dad was singing in the choir at the back but she didn't even dare turn around to wave, as the last time she tried this, he was cross with her for misbehaving.

Martha twiddled a penny piece round and round in her pocket, transferring it from one pocket to the other, as she waited for the collection plate to come. She accidentally dropped it. The penny rolled under the bench in front and disappeared. Martha dropped down on all fours, twisting and turning to try and spy the coin. 'Leave it. Get up,' whispered Mary. More heads in front ducked as other worshipers searched. Two rows in front, the treasured coin was found and passed back to a beaming Martha and a relieved Mary.
'Don't lose it again and sit still,' breathed Mary, as Martha wriggled restlessly from side to side.

'Emma's knocking me,' whined Martha.
'I'm bored,' sighed Emma.
'Shut up,' whispered Tim.

Mary raised her eyes upwards and prayed to God to take over the supervision, as she felt so frustrated. Being a convert to Catholicism, she was very serious in her prayers and liked to follow every word and movement. It was difficult with the spoken words in Latin and although Mary had the English translation in her Mass book, she was not too familiar with all the actions and words. Having to contend with three bored children did nothing for her religious fervour. At last it was the final hymn. The priest and altar boys filed off the sanctuary. The congregation waited for the strains of music to die away before the shuffling and whispering began.

'Can I go and light a candle?' asked Martha. Mary groped in her pocket for coins so that Emma could put a penny in the candle money box. Yesterday Tom sold two dozen eggs to the postman so that they could have some church collection money but this was dwindling fast. Mary found some pennies.
'Here, Tim. One for Emma too but don't let her light the candle. She's too little and might burn herself.' The children squeezed past her and went over to the candle stand but not before Tim grabbed Emma's coat and dragged her almost to her knees.
'You should genuflect like this,' he demonstrated, in his big-brotherly way.
'Now Martha's won me,' retorted Emma as she pushed at Tim and ran to Martha. Mary, witnessing all this, sighed again. She hoped someone up above understood the ways of little ones. She picked up her bag and joined her children as they knelt with hands clasped and eyes closed before the flickering lights.

They got up and walked to the back of the church.
'I want to dip my finger, Mammy,' shouted Emma. Before Mary had time to answer, a pair of arms reached down and lifted Emma within reach of the water stoup.
'There you are, lassie,' said the man holding her. Emma was delighted.
'Mr Netherfield, isn't it?' Mary asked, offering her hand.
'That's right,' he replied, his warm hand not as rough and callused as Tom's. 'We met at Moorhouses' sale. Settling in okay?'

'Well, I'm beginning to, but it's been a long, hard winter and lonely on my own all day with the children.'

'I'll have to see what I can do about that, seeing as we are neighbours,' responded Mr Netherfield. Mary smiled. He was a bit different to the other farmers she met. His speech was more refined and he was interested in conversation other than about the weather. She was flattered at the personal interest. They walked down the pathway and joined other parishioners. The men were forming a group on the opposite side of the road to the ladies as was customary. Jack Netherfield smiled at Mary and crossed over the road.

For many of these folk, it was the social meeting of the week where they exchanged news and views on the week's goings-on and inevitably the weather. The next half hour seemed to pass by quickly before people slowly dispersed, many on foot and a few in cars or trucks. Tom sauntered up the village with his friends and acquaintances. He'd enjoyed his chat but was feeling a little uneasy after spotting the almost intimate exchanges of smiles between his wife and Jack Netherfield. Tom knew Jack Netherfield lived alone, and that there were other pretty, young, single lasses around.

'Why take such an interest in Mary?' he thought. 'Mary's a very attractive woman but married and heavily pregnant.' There was something about this neighbour that troubled him. 'Maybe I'm overreacting,' Tom thought, and with that, he dismissed the idea, as he sauntered into Hunters Lodge.

Mary, meanwhile, with the children, walked to the Post Office and General Dealers, the only shop in the village. It was open on Sunday mornings for the outlying farmers to buy their Farmer's Weekly. The children spent some considerable time getting value for money over the counter, as Mrs Stoutly, a large, jovial, round-faced, grey-haired woman, chatted with Mary. Jack Stoutly was as round and as pleasant as his wife. He beamed down on the three Holmes children.

'Coming on fine they are,' he said. 'Bonny little things, aren't they? You're going to have your hands full with another one, I see.'

Mary nodded and smiled. She ushered her children out and they walked to Hunters Lodge, a little further up the road.

'Has dad gone in for a drink?' asked Tim, hoping that this meant a drink of lemonade for him and the girls.

'Yes, he has. Stay there. I'll be back in a minute. Tim, just watch them for two seconds,' Mary instructed. The children waited on a stretch of open grass outside the public house, trying to peer through the windows. A little later, Mary brought out lemonade for the children. 'Don't spill it. Dad won't be long.'

What was in fact less than half an hour seemed an age to the children. Having quickly downed their drinks and eaten their sweets, they played around on the grass near the public house door, hoping that their dad would soon come out. Mary sat on the wooden bench, watching them play.

'I wish we could go in,' sighed Tim, as he heard laughter and talking and saw various men come and go. It seemed to him a very exciting place to be. He knew that his dad would be in fine fettle when he came out.

'Just a few more minutes,' Tom had shouted after her.

Mary was ready for home. After a further wait, she took the children by the hands and led them through the smoky, beery atmosphere of the bar to the back yard ready for their transport, such as it was. Tom, seeing her with the children, downed the last dregs of beer from his glass and followed her out. He went to the stables and brought Drummer out and yoked him up and the family climbed into the cart. Tom was in good form as Tim had anticipated. Drummer pulled away from Hunters Lodge to the strains of *Oh Danny Boy* being rendered in full voice by Tom. It has been a very enjoyable trip for Mary too but she knew that soon she would be back to her lonely life on the farm.

'I wonder,' she thought, 'will it ever get any better? Maybe that neighbour, Mr Netherfield, will call in for a chat to ease the loneliness.'

The days passed. They seemed long to Mary. Her swollen tummy was heavy to carry as she slowly waddled around. Her back ached as she leaned backwards to spread the weight. She was up early each day to light the fire. She was finding housework irksome but was pleased with the bright, sunny days as the washing dried outside even though she found hanging it out, hard work.

'It's so back-aching,' she thought one day as she stopped and stared at the basket load at her feet, rubbing her lower back with both hands. 'Is that you, Tom?' she asked, as she heard footsteps approaching. She thought Tom was away in the fields and was surprised to hear him coming.

'No,' responded another voice. Mary turned around.

'Hello again, Mr Netherfield. I thought you were Tom.' Mary smiled at him. Jack gently took hold of her shoulders.

'Let me finish hanging these out for you. Sit down over there by that tree and rest yourself a while,' he said, kindly, leading her towards the tree. Mary, feeling so weary, allowed herself to be helped to sit down and then watched whilst Jack adeptly hung the washing on the line.

After he finished, he sat down on the grass beside her and brought out his cigarettes.

'Here, have one of these. Enjoy the break.' They chatted quietly together for no more than ten minutes about farming and such before the girls came running up.

'Hello,' they chorused to Jack.

'Hello, girls,' he replied, getting to his feet, and looking at Mary, said, 'I'll be going now. See you again. Look after yourself.' Mary watched, for a moment, his tall, lean frame taken easily by his long strides until he disappeared over the bank.

'You seem in good fettle today, lass,' remarked Tom, after teatime. 'Had a good day, have you?' Before Mary could answer, Martha piped up.

'That nice man came today, the one who lifted Emma up in church, didn't he, Mammy? Mammy had a cigarette with him in garden,' she continued, quite innocently. Tom looked up at Mary in surprise as she continued washing the pots.

'Jack Netherfield? What did he want?'

'I don't know really. He never said. Just being neighbourly, I suppose. Probably passing through and called in to see how we were doing,' said Mary, nonchalantly.

'It seems reasonable enough,' acknowledged Tom to himself, whilst feeling a little uncomfortable. He could have sworn it was Jack Netherfield walking by the beck when he was going over to Charlie's. 'Why would he come calling when surely he recognised Drummer and cart heading in the other direction? Maybe I'll go calling on him one day,' he thought, the hairs on the back of his neck bristling. He put the incident to the back of his mind.

The following Saturday evening, Mary performed the usual ritual of bringing the deep, oval, tin bath that hung from a nail in the stone wall of the wash house, into the kitchen in front of the fire. The water in the copper by the fire was hot. She filled a bucketful and poured it into the bath. She went into the wash house and filled the bucket with cold water, carried it into the kitchen and added some to the bath water. A tin jug of lukewarm water mixed by Mary was on standby to rinse the suds from the children's hair. It was an effort for Mary with all the lifting and carrying, as the copper had to be refilled, also from the wash house tap. As she was filling the bath with water, she felt a sudden twinge.

'It has to come sometime,' she thought. 'Hopefully it will be tonight while the children are in bed.'

'Emma, Martha,' she called, as she took from a drawer their clean nightdresses, second hand from better off relatives and a bit thin, but that did not worry the girls. Sometimes they wore Tom's old shirts, anything to keep them warm. Mary went through the nightly routine as normal. The girls were stripped and bathed and each had her hair washed and briskly rubbed dry. They curled up on the mat in their faded, flowered nightdresses, their dark hair shining like silk.

Mary stopped in her tracks and drew in her breath as another contraction took hold.

'All to go through again,' she thought, and felt frightened and yet relieved. She didn't want the pain that she knew was ahead but she had become very weary lately and it would be lovely to be slim again.

'Any milk needed?' shouted Tom, from the wash house.

'No thanks, love, but you might empty me this bath before you go out.'

'Where's Tim?' asked Tom, as he strode in and picked up the tin bath. 'I need a hand.' He watched Mary lean over the table and gasp and his face showed concern. 'How long is it going to be, lass?' he asked, anxiously.

'Get away and get your milking done. It'll be sometime yet,' she replied, the tears spilling down her cheeks.

'Come on lass. Don't cry,' consoled Tom, gently caressing her. 'I'll be as quick as I can.'

Greener beyond the hill

Emma and Martha were engrossed in a game of cards, but one that only tots could create where the rules and the aim of the game were made up as they went along. They were very much occupied and not aware of the drama that was about to take place.

'Will you come out t' lav with me, Emma?' asked Martha.

'Put your coats on,' ordered Mary. 'You've just been in the bath.' The little girls pulled on their boots and old coats, and trudged around the corner of the house to the lavatory. They were quite used to the wooden seat, the cobwebs in the corners of the brick walls, and the spiders and beetles that scurried about. They took their time and wandered back, knowing they would be chased off to bed.

'Say your prayers now,' Mary said, after they had washed their hands. The three of them knelt on the mat, Mary with a little one at each side of her and they prayed.

'God bless mammy and daddy,' they chanted, and added, 'and Tim and Martha and Emma.' The two girls repeated Mary's words with eyes screwed tightly shut and hands joined together. 'And keep us safe till morning light. Amen.'

'I want a drink please, Mammy,' said Martha, jumping to her feet.

'Quickly, then,' and as another pain engulfed her, she could only stay kneeling, gripping the nearest chair. As the contraction passed over, Mary heaved herself up. 'Goodnight. God bless. You go up yourselves tonight. Mammy's tired.' Martha and Emma went quietly to bed.

Mary paddled about and wandered in and out. She tidied up and made the preparations for the new arrival. A knock at the door brought her out of her preoccupation. She opened it to greet Dorothy who had received a message from Tom via Tim.

'Just come to sit with you for a while.'

'Thanks, Dorothy, but I warn you, I'm not much company. You could help me make the bed up, though.' Earlier in the week, in readiness for the birth, Tom had dismantled their bed and carried it downstairs to the sitting room with Charlie's help when he'd called to discuss a problem with one of his cows.

'Right. We'll do that and then we'll have a nice cup of tea,' replied Dorothy. She filled the kettle and put it on the fire to boil. Mary knew it was going to be a long night. After making the bed ready, Mary mooched around the kitchen whilst Dorothy made the tea.

Mary drank a little from her cup but couldn't settle. She paced up and down, only stopping for another pain.

'I'll just wander down to the cowshed a minute and see Tom,' she said to Dorothy.

'All right, lass. I'll stay here and listen out for bairns.'

Mary made her way outside and leant against a wall.

'Oh, God,' she thought. 'Why don't I remember it's like this,' breathing deeply until the pain subsided. She wandered down the cobbles. She could hear whistling from the cowshed but she continued, walking past the cowshed door and onto the track.

'Where can I go?' she thought. 'I can't do this again.' Her back felt as if it was being stretched in two. The pains were more frequent.

'Mary,' called Tom, with concern showing in his voice, having come out of the cowshed and spotting her further along the track. He walked quickly towards her. Putting his arm around her shoulders, he guided her back to the house.

'Drink this,' said Dorothy, handing a hot mug of tea to Mary as Tom led her into the kitchen.

'I'd better go t' village and phone doctor,' Tom said to Dorothy. 'I'll not be long.' He went at a rapid pace over the moor and down into Windrush village and made his way into Hunters Lodge. 'Just a quick one,' he said to Ben Edwards, 'and can I use your phone please. Missus is on way.' A few farmers sitting nearby looked up as he said this. Among them was Jack Netherfield. Tom made his phone call, downed his pint and set off for home.

Time ticked by. There was no easing of pain for Mary. She thought it might get easier having had three babies but it didn't seem to be. She wandered into the sitting room, now their bedroom and tried to relax but couldn't. Why didn't she remember what it was like? Why was she in this situation again. She vividly recalled the previous birth and those utterings of Nurse Hampson when in labour with Emma and about to push.

'Come on, my dearie. Just try a little harder. It will soon all be over,' the midwife said. Mary knew she was encouraging her with well-worn words but it did little to reassure her that the birth was imminent. It seemed so long, thought Mary, so wearying on that blazing-hot July day in nineteen-forty. She remembered enviously eyeing Nurse Hampson, sitting in the well-worn wicker chair, relaxed and comfortable, chain-smoking. Spirals of smoke slowly spread into a haze and clouded the small attic bedroom of the stone-built cottage but the elderly midwife seemed oblivious. Mary had a clear picture in her mind of Nurse Hampson, short in stature and overweight. Her leathery skin was wrinkled and on her chin, were numbers of wiry, grey hairs protruding from a mole. The nurse told Mary that she spent many hours puffing and blowing the smoke while waiting for babies. She told Mary she was almost immune to the groans of mothers-to-be and was looking forward to returning to her comfortable small house in the nearby village rather than sitting in a draughty, cold and spartan cottage. However, she'd been sympathetic towards Mary who was growing weary after hours of a distressing labour.

Mary re-lived those next few intense final moments. She remembered glimpsing through the half-drawn curtains, a beautiful, blue sky with shafts of brilliant sunlight falling across the home-made patterned quilt loosely laid over the bed. A great longing to escape had filled her mind as another pain engulfed her. 'Could I,' she pondered, 'could I just leap from this bed and out of the open window, across the green fields and away, away from this pain?' She thought of the desperate prayer, 'please God, help me,' she'd made and with greater urgency, repeating her plea. Then with added strength, she bore down yet again and her whole body seemed to open to expel into the harsh glare of light, a baby girl with a mass of black hair. The baby cried a newborn squeaky noise.

'Is she all right?' Mary remembered asking the nurse.
'She's got all her fingers and toes if that's what you mean,' was Nurse Hampson's forthright reply. After cutting the cord, the nurse wrapped the baby in a piece of sheeting, placing her in an emptied open drawer taken from the bedroom chest of drawers in readiness. The placenta that followed the delivery was rolled up in layers of the newspaper on which Mary had delivered, ready for burning on the open fire downstairs along with the bloodied old sheeting. The dark, ruddy-brown, thick, rubber sheeting brought by the nurse was removed from under Mary and placed in the bag for cleaning later. Having made the mother comfortable, Nurse Hampson, efficient as ever, poured water from an old, chipped water jug, ready prepared when she had realised the baby was soon to be

born, into a matching bowl and dipped in her elbow, to test the temperature before immersing the squawking baby to wash her. She chatted continuously as she dried and clothed the baby and, as Mary thought, was trying to be positive in such dismal surroundings, with her comment that, 'I love the open view from the window.'

'It is a lovely cottage with having such a view,' thought Mary, trying to look on the bright side.

Mary came back to the present as another pain grew in intensity around her back. As it subsided, she paddled back to the kitchen. Dorothy smiled. At midnight, Doctor Mosey came walking in. He was a short, dumpy fellow with big, bushy eyebrows and huge hands.

'We'll have you on the bed, please, Mrs Holmes, and see what's happening,' he said, following Mary into the sitting room. A little later, Dr Mosey came out. 'I'll hang around,' he said to Tom. 'I think it will be here in the early hours and it feels like a big one.' Tom nodded.

'Mind if I see Dorothy home?' Tom asked him. Dorothy found it a bit eerie in the pitch blackness with only a torch to light the way. 'No, you go. You have plenty of time for that.' The doctor settled himself down in Tom's armchair whilst Tom walked with Dorothy over to Crossbeck farm.

'I'll look in over next few days, Tom, to give you a hand,' Dorothy said, on arriving at her door.'

'Thanks, Dorothy. That will be great.'

In the early hours, around half past one, Dr Mosey was checking on Mary. 'Not long now, Mrs Holmes.' Mary was groaning. Her whole body seemed to be immersed in pain. 'I think you're about ready for pushing.' Mary gave a long, low moan that grew in crescendo. 'You're doing fine. It's a big one. Give another push.' Mary reached out to grip the bed frame as she tried to expel this baby into the world. 'Push! Now pant,' Dr Mosey instructed as he gently eased out the head. 'One more push and we'll have your baby.'

'I can't,' Mary cried. 'I can't. Oh God!' She dug her teeth into her bottom lip and her feet into the bed and pushed. Dr Mosey eased out the shoulders and the baby was there.

'He's a big ten pounder, I'd guess. A great big lad,' he said.

It was two o'clock and a bit early for the cockerel to herald the birth with its shrill calls. Mary was exhausted but raised a weak smile for Tom. She knew he was pleased to get another son. 'Mark,' stated Mary. 'That's what we'll call him, eh, Tom? Mark, you know, up with the lark, well almost,' she added, weakly. 'It's fine by me, lass. Won't little lasses and Tim be surprised in morning?' Mark bawled and screwed up his big, round eyes. His skin was beautiful and smooth for a newly born baby. He gazed around the bedroom almost as if he were sizing up his new surroundings, the pale blue distemper peeling off the wall in parts; the low brown beams stretching from corner to corner with laced cobwebs splayed across from beam to beam; and the fire crackling in the tiny fireplace along the far wall. Dr Mosey washed the baby, after seeing to Mary. Tom took the bloodied sheet used for the birth into the wash house in a bucket to soak, after removing all the sodden paper to smoulder and burn on the kitchen fire. Mary cradled Mark in her arms and gazed at his tiny face. 'Another little miracle,' she thought. It always filled her with awe, this wonder of birth. Tom brought her a mug of tea and gave one to Dr Mosey who gratefully acknowledged it.

Later, after seeing the doctor to the first gate, having given him almost all the eggs he could find, as thanks for such dedication and help and promising the doctor some cuttings or a piece of bacon from his next killed pig, as a further payment, Tom sank wearily into his armchair. 'One last woodbine,' he thought, 'before sleep.' He pondered. 'Different at night,' he recalled, resting his eyes and looking back at the day almost three years ago, when Emma was born.

He remembered eagerly making his way home on that beautiful summer's day in July, striding purposefully across the field into the cottage. Tim, lean and dark like Tom, flung himself into his daddy's arms and shouted the news whilst Martha, dark-haired and brown-eyed like Mary, wriggled across the stone floor on her belly, her fat little bottom going from side to side as she dragged herself to her daddy's feet. Tom took her into his arms and, pulling off his smelly, dirty wellingtons, padded in his well-darned socks up the bare, wooden stairs, calling for Tim to follow. The children did not mind the scruffy overalls that were evident of his daily work. Tim's chatter, Martha's squeals of delight and the new baby's cries filled the tiny cottage. Tom gently placed his children on the linoleum-covered floor. For a moment, the world stood still as he and Mary gazed at their latest, tiny offspring.

'Such a beautiful baby,' he thought. 'You've done it again, lass,' he said, tenderly. 'She's a topper. You've come up trumps.' Mary smiled a silent prayer of thanks.

'I'll go now, Tom,' called Milly, their elderly neighbour, who occupied an adjoining cottage. 'I'll be in again tomorrow.' Milly, tall and thin with lined forehead, her straggly, grey hair tied back in a bun and crow's feet aside her smiling eyes, was a gentle person with a caring nature and kindly face. She promised to spend time looking after Tim and Martha whilst Tom was at work, until Mary was back on her feet. Tom made his way downstairs with the older two. 'There's a package burning on the fire,' she said to Tom, meeting his eyes with a knowing look. 'Just keep an eye on it. It's a bit messy. You know, the one the nurse gave me when she left.' Tom grasped her meaning.

'Thanks a lot, Milly,' he said, showing her to the door. 'Don't know what I'd do without you.'

Tom stirred from his reminiscing and moved. The ash from his smouldering cigarette was lengthening and his movement dislodged it. Dusting it down from his overalls, he threw the remainder of the cigarette into the embers of the fire.

'Not much point getting undressed,' he thought. It was four o'clock in the morning and he would soon be out milking after supervising the little ones on their early rising. Tom placed a few more coals on the fire and had a quick peep at his wife and son, now both sleeping peacefully. He thankfully eased off his boots and settled down to try and snatch some sleep before the next demanding day was upon him but his mind was restless. 'We've really struggled to make it through this first winter at Bankside,' he thought. 'I wonder how Mary will cope with another baby when I'm busy on farm. It will be hard going financially. I wonder will we be able to keep going.'

Greener beyond the hill

1943 Summer Autumn

Mary opened the coals door and looked out onto the valley early one morning in summer.

'It's beautiful,' she thought. 'It's such a tranquil, peaceful place.' It was. Mists were rolling slowly down the valley giving it a ghostly appearance. The pale of the clouds was a sharp contrast to the vibrant-green, lush grass. Soon the mists would lift to reveal the farms lying in the sun and the cows munching on the pastures. Mary was beginning to love Moorbeck. Later, she wheeled out Mark in his dilapidated pram to sleep in the orchard. Mary's depression, which oppressed her throughout the dark winter months, was being replaced by a sense of calm and joy.

The two older children joined Tim in the cowshed watching him milking. They often made their way along the cobbles to where he was working in the sheds, finding it fascinating to see him sitting under a cow, squirting milk into a bucket. Cows, however, have no use for little children, as Martha discovered. She was totally immersed in thought at the wonder of these animals, but suddenly stepped back when a cow, having no respect for time or place, swished up its tail and released a torrent. Martha had never seen such a cascade of water. She was mesmerised. Tom with his lovely velvet singing voice, often burst forth into tenor or bass while milking, assuring his children that the cows loved his music. The children were so utterly convinced that he was right in all that he said, that they believed him. On many a morning, the musical strains drifted from beyond the open wooden door as Tim and Martha joined Tom in song. This, they, thought, helped to increase the milk yield from the cows. Emma usually stayed in the house with baby Mark.

Martha bent down to stroke the two cats. Smokey, the very old, black one, left by the previous owners, was no longer much of a mouse catcher but was a friendly, lazy pet for the youngsters to stroke without fear. Ginger was quick and frisky. Both were waiting patiently for their ration of milk to be poured into the hewn-out brick. This was part of a ritual for Tom who fed the cats each morning and evening. They loved the warm milk. No animal, if useful, was too small or insignificant for him to care for. It was to his advantage if his cats were healthy, as they could keep down the mice that ran freely in and out of the old, brick buildings.

'Don't they sing loudly when they drink the milk, Daddy,' commented Martha.

'Purr, silly,' stated Tim. 'Cats purr, don't they, Daddy?' he added, looking up to him. Tom glanced at Martha who wore an old, cotton dress and a faded, blue cardigan with many buttons missing. Her little fat knees peeped out over her boots.

'She is a picture,' thought Tom, and waves of pride and tenderness swept over him as he answered Tim's question. His children might look like little waifs and strays to others, but to Tom they were his beautiful princesses and his handsome prince.

'Grand mug of tea that, lad, tell your mam,' Tom said to Tim, who brought the early morning brew across the cobbles from the house, leaving Mary busy with Mark and preparing the table ready for breakfast. Tim opened his mouth to reply, and like a flash of lightening, a jet of milk shot across the cowshed and found its mark. Tim spluttered and laughed.

'Dad, stop it,' he gasped, but the milk was being squirted back into the bucket. Tom grinned. He could not resist a little light relief in his busy day.

'Your face was a picture, lad. Good stuff though, isn't it?' Tim nodded and grinned.

The next moment disaster occurred. Martha, standing with her back to the large, warm body of Beauty, slipped and fell, landing face down underneath the cow. Reaction was quick. Beauty, often irritated by the ginger kitten running in and out of her legs, was used to giving a swipe at it with one of her hooves. She did so this time at Martha. As the little girl lay on the cement floor, motionless from the knock, the beast raised its hoof and paddled on her, leaving the hoof firmly planted on her tiny back. The cow turned its head around and stared with baleful eyes at this cumbersome object that was trapped under its foot. This all happened in seconds, and far too quickly for Tom to prevent it. He leaped from his three-legged stool, dropping his pail, half full of precious milk. He bent under the cow, heaving her over with his body. He lifted her hoof from Martha's back and slid his hands under the limp body of his daughter. A stream of angry words passed from his lips to the docile cow.

Still cursing and swearing and with Tim running behind him, Tom carried Martha to the house and laid her very gently on the faded, brown sofa. She was deathly pale and still.

'What's happened? Oh, look at her head. Oh, dear. Oh, Tom!' shrieked Mary. An enormous bruise was appearing on Martha's forehead, emphasising her ghostly, white face against her silky, black hair.

'I'm more worried about her back,' replied Tom, anxiously watching Martha with a comforting arm around his wife's shoulder. 'Keep her warm and rested. I'll have to get finished. I won't be long. I'm sure she'll come to, in a little while. Send Tim if you need me.' He strode out again, stiffly, his body tense with anger and worry.

'Will she die, Mammy?' questioned Tim.

'No, no, darling. She's sleeping. You say a little prayer to God to keep her all right,' replied Mary, reassuringly, but inside she was feeling sick with worry. She laid a blanket over Martha and went to pick up Mark. Emma sidled to the sofa and perched on the end, gazing at her motionless sister. Mary kept glancing over to Martha whilst feeding Mark and at intervals, got up to see if she was still breathing. Mary felt very uneasy. 'Go and ask your daddy how long he'll be,' she said to Tim. A few minutes later, Tom appeared at the door.

'I'm about done milking. How is she?'

'I think you should ring the doctor?' said Mary, her lips trembling as she spoke. 'I'm worried. She hasn't moved and the swelling is getting worse.'

'That's bruising coming out. That's a good sign. Put some cold cloths on it and keep an eye on her. I'll let cows out and swill out later. I'll send Tim over to Charlie's to ask if he'll take milk this morning and I'll go to phone in village.' He went out. Mary settled Mark and kept vigil with Emma. No one was interested in breakfast.

It seemed an age before Tom returned.

'Ambulance is coming. They want her in hospital to check her out.' Mary burst into tears. 'It's for best, lass. She'll be okay.' He went back out to clean the cowshed. Mary made some tea and tried to eat. She kept going to the door to see if the ambulance was in sight. There was no change in Martha. She just lay there. No movement at all.

'She could be dead,' thought Mary, but Martha was still breathing. Mary went to the door again. She could hear a distant rumbling and knew a vehicle was on its way down the bank. She saw Tim running to open the gate at the bottom of the bank. Her eyes filled up. Shortly, Tom entered the kitchen with the driver and his assistant.

'Anyone coming with her?' the driver asked. Mary and Tom looked at each other.

'Will she be staying in?' asked Tom.

'I would think so, overnight anyway.

'You can't go, Tom. I'll have to,' Mary said, and turning to the driver, added, 'I must take my baby. I'm feeding him myself.'

'Yes, bring your baby. Let's get this little one into the ambulance.' Mary was soon ready. Tom picked up Emma to hold her as the ambulance pulled away. Tim had already walked on to the gate to open it for them.

The house seemed empty without Mary, Martha and little Mark. Tom knew he wouldn't get to see Mary that night as there was enough to do looking after his two children and doing farm jobs. Tom was restless and anxious all evening. He and Mary normally listened to the play on the wireless on a Saturday night but tonight Tom was not interested. The picture of Martha under the cow kept flooding his mind. He could feel her limp body in his arms. Tom sat and smoked endless woodbines before finally going up to bed.

Next morning, after milking, Tom took his two children down to Windrush to church, as it was Sunday. He called in at Hunters Lodge to leave Drummer and asked Ben if he could make a phone call.

'I want to see how they're getting on,' he said, after explaining the events.

Meanwhile, Mary spent the night dozing in an armchair by the side of Martha's bed in the small hospital room. Mark mostly slept between feeds. He was a placid baby. The nurses were wonderful but it seemed they were in and out all night long, doing tests and checks. It was about nine o'clock next morning, when Martha opened her eyes. She looked dazed but immediately recognised Mary and held out her arms.

'Thank God,' said Mary. 'Oh, Martha, my precious.' She hugged her little girl tightly as tears of relief flowed freely down her cheeks. It was another hour before the doctor decided that Martha could go home. She had suffered concussion and much bruising but there was no permanent damage. The nurse came in to say that Tom had been on the phone.

'Did you tell him we're coming home?' asked Mary.

'Yes, I did. He sounded very relieved.' Martha spent the next few days on the sofa resting. She was very shaken up and quiet, not even wanting to play with Emma. It was days before she returned to the cowshed as her faith in the docile animals was shaken and she was more than a little afraid. It was a fear that took her a long time to overcome.

September arrived. It was a bright, sunny morning. Tim was standing by the cart house with his shoulders squared and his sandwiches in a box carefully packed inside a bag hanging on his back. He was waiting for Charlie.

'School at last and a great day in his life,' thought Mary. She was feeling sad as she stood by the coals door with Emma by her side, to see her first child take this important stop into the outside world without her to watch over him. 'He seems so small,' she thought, as he stood there waiting patiently for Charlie to take him along with Charlie's daughter, May, to St Peter's school in Windrush, delivering the milk churns on the way. The horse and cart arrived. Tim waited whilst Tom's milk churn was lifted on to the cart alongside Charlie's and secured with rope, before scrambling up and holding on to the rope. Tim was careful not to stand too near the churns because when the cart jolted, milk splashed out from under the churn lids. As the horse set off, Tim turned to wave a last goodbye to his mam and Emma and again to his dad who was watching from the door of the cowshed with Martha.

'He seems such a young lad to face the long day with new playmates and new surroundings,' thought Tom. He was proud that Tim was showing no emotional upset and seemed keen to go to school.

May said little to Tim. The same likeness was there, the same dark, straight hair and thick, dark eyebrows but May was quiet and rather sullen-looking, unlike Tim who stared eagerly around him, his bright eyes watching everything that went on. On arriving at the milk stand, a makeshift wooden platform made from an old trailer, Charlie untied the rope and heaved on to it the full milk churns, placing them alongside the churns from other outlying farms, as he was the last farmer to arrive. He picked up his empties and fastened them securely in his cart and was only just in time as the milk lorry arrived and pulled up beside the stand. Charlie guided his horse around the milk lorry and made his way along the tarmac road, turning left at the Windrush signpost, to make the last mile into the village.

St Peter's school was run by one elderly teacher, Mrs Featherstone. She was tall, thin with pointed features and her glasses perched low on her nose, making her appearance rather foreboding in the eyes of her young pupils. She'd taught the village children for many years, but it was not easy to instil into children the facts and figures that needed to be learnt, when they were basically concerned with the land and life of animals. Pushing wisps of greying hair back into place in a tight bun at the nape of her neck, she greeted Tim kindly. She knew his father was from a local farming family and that Tom's schooling until fourteen years of age, was very basic. From the few times that she met Mary, she was of the impression that Mary was an intelligent woman, even though Mary had told her she left school at an early age. As Mrs Featherstone ushered Tim to a chair, she was fervently hoping that here perhaps, was a future successful candidate of the eleven plus examination as no pupil from the school passed it the last three years and she could see little hope of success in the up and coming pupils.

Tim was eyed by a handful of children sitting in rows behind their wooden desks or tables. Toby, a big, broad child with a simple nature, leaned over to him.
'You walked here?' he questioned. Tim shook his head. 'You 'ad a ride?' Tim nodded. 'You ride 'ome?' the questioning continued.
'No.'
'You walk?' persisted Toby
'Yes.'
'Our Toby, sit down,' called his older brother Phil, a short, squat lad with untidy, wavy, brown hair and wearing a jacket, a size too small. Mrs Featherstone manoeuvred stiffly behind her desk next to the fire crackling in the corner of the classroom. Tim eyed the

cane lying along the desk next to the register and his heart beat faster.

Martha wandered aimlessly around during the day with her younger sister, her big brown eyes looking sorrowful. She was missing her brother very much.

'What's matter with you Martha?' questioned Mary.

'He's been a long time,' Martha kept saying. 'I have to feed hens tonight and gather eggs, as daddy says Tim will be tired after his first day but I think he's lucky, missing doing all his jobs.' Emma could not see why Martha was so miserable. Emma was her usual energetic self and quite willing to have a go at anything. She enjoyed helping.

'I'll help you with the eggs, Martha,' she said, enthusiastically.

'No, you might drop them.'

'I won't.' They stood in their boots and slightly too large, hand-me-down clothes, with their hair clipped back. Mary spied them, nattering away to each other like two little old women, she thought. Martha and Emma were often sent out to play on a fine day as Mary needed rest and quiet whenever possible due to night time feeding Mark. He was taking longer than her other children to last the night without a feed. The girls spent hours wandering around the farm playing make-believe games of mammies and daddies or Joe and Jack, two old farmers.

Tom had overheard them and related it to Mary.

'You should hear them,' he recounted. 'There's Martha saying, *I'm old Jack and you're old Joe and you come and tell me your cow's bad and I come and help.* Emma obeys, of course,' he added. 'She looks up to her elder sister and is quite happy to follow her instructions. They have all sorts of pretend games going on when those two heads get together.' The girls were in the throes of another of their pretend games, when they were brought back to reality by the familiar sing-song noise of

'Ooo, Ooo, Ooo, Ooo,' echoing in highs and lows from the coals door.

'That's mammy calling daddy. Tea's ready,' said Martha. Emma heard it too. It was like an Indian love call that Mary used when she needed to contact Tom. The high-pitched sound rang out across the fields to where he was working, and his deeper

'Ooo, Ooo, Ooo, Ooo,' floated back through the air, message received and understood.

Meanwhile Tim finished his first day at school but it was a long walk home.
'Tarra,' Tim said to May when they reached the turn-off to Bankside farmhouse. His legs ached and he was glad to be home. As he trudged into the house, he was plagued with questions from Martha.
'What was it like? What did you do?'
'Hello, Mammy, I'm tired. What's for tea?' was Tim's reply.
Tom's footsteps were heard out on the cobbles. He strode in, removed his flat cap and hung it on a nail on the low wooden-beamed ceiling.
'Now lad, had a good day? How's it been?'
'All right, Daddy, I suppose, but I'd just as soon stay and help you.'
'Now you stick in and learn, lad.'

Tom turned to his wife. 'Did you have a rest, lass? I saw little ones were out.' Tom bent over and kissed his wife. Martha smiled and Emma beamed on hearing the reference to them by Tom as they stood at the table waiting to eat their tea. Emma found it difficult reaching the table even when standing. Tom was intending to go to the salesrooms in Whitby to pick up some cheap chairs when he could find the time. Apart from his old, wooden armchair and Mary's rocking chair, there was only one other hard chair which Tim claimed, being the eldest. It wasn't long before the children were tucked up in bed, Tim having coped well with his first day at school, much to Mary's relief.

'Another of those nights,' thought Mary, one evening, a week or two later, watching Tom, dressed in his Home Guard uniform, taking his heavy greatcoat from behind the door. When the Home Guard was formed in nineteen-forty by those in reserved occupation including farmers, to act as a defence force, uniform was in short supply. Eventually there was enough and it included a greatcoat and strong boots, much to Tom's delight as the coat was very warm.

'It's a bit chilly tonight,' Tom stated, putting on the coat, 'and that hall is a draughty old place.' He picked up his gun, having previously explained to his wife that they trained during the evenings in such things as weapon handling, unarmed combat and basic sabotage. Some members, when training, used a pike which was an obsolete bayonet welded onto a metal pole. This was a War Office issue due to shortage of ammunition despite the appeal to the public to hand in their shotguns and pistols which had brought in a good quantity of guns.

At night, in some areas, members patrolled the fields in which enemy gliders or paratroops might land, and the men wanted to be ready for them. Tom said that it was important to be ready to defend roads and villages to block enemy movement and as units knew who lived locally, they could check the identity cards of any strangers. Mary appreciated that the aim of the Home Guard in the event of an invasion, was to try and slow down the advance of the enemy, even if by a few hours, to give regular troops time to regroup, thus making these meetings well worth attending. Tom hadn't been able to get to many up to now. However, Charlie, having recently bought a van, was picking him up.

'That'll be Charlie,' said Tom, on hearing knocking at the door. 'I don't know what time I'll be back. Don't wait up.' He gave his wife a kiss and walked out. Mary smiled.
'And it will be a few pints in the pub afterwards,' she thought, switching on the wireless. 'Maybe I'll find something to listen to and have a quiet night, hopefully, if Mark doesn't wake up.' She never heard Tom come to bed but he told her next day that it had been a long night.

Summer crept into autumn. The sunshine disappeared. There was no escape from the poverty at Bankside. The idyllic conditions of summer in this sunny valley and a carefree disposition brought an unrealistic sense of wellbeing, but with colder evenings and greyer days, the stark reality of facing another winter of hardship was already dawning in Tom's mind. One or two cows were in calf. The milk yield would increase in the following spring when they calved, he reckoned. Daisy, the cart horse mare, was in foal, but Tom's luck ran out with two of his cows, one of which suffered from mastitis quite badly and was of no more use to him. Another died before the vet could work on a cure and the vet's bills were a heavy drain on his slender budget. Tom understood that farmers invariably coped with ups and downs, but disappointments were hard to take. He knew Mary was struggling to feed their growing children, and was unable to buy any extras for the family. With these thoughts in mind, he began walking out in the late evening with his gun and Trigger waylaying any unsuspecting rabbits. Not only did they provide a nourishing meal the next day and soup the day after, but if enough were shot, he could take them to Whitby to sell.

One dusky evening, walking quietly alongside the front field and up towards the sand hole field, he recalled Martha telling him about the baby rabbits.

'You know, Daddy,' she said, one day over tea in late summer, her bright, little face, full of animation and expression, 'Emma and me, we crawled on our knees up t' sand hole today, and we laid on our tummies and kept quiet. Do you know, Daddy, lots of little rabbits kept coming out of holes and playing and running around? They were lovely, Daddy. It must be a great, big house they have under that sand.' Tom laughed at the time. The sand hole was a big patch of sandy gravel, half under the hill in the corner of the field, with a rabbit warren underneath.

'Breeding like rabbits is a good expression,' he thought. 'Thank God for rabbits. They are going to be some of our bread and butter this winter in more ways than one.' He sat in the hedgerow, lit a woodbine, and waited. Then he spotted them, the rosehips. He could sell them in Whitby along with the rabbits. Every penny would help and pennies made shillings.

A few days later, he put his thoughts into action.

'Come on, bairns,' he shouted. 'We're ready.' It was the following Saturday afternoon when Tom decided to go rosehip picking. Armed with bags, Mary by his side and Mark in the pram, he was waiting impatiently for the three children to appear. Martha and Emma came running up, followed by Tim, each carrying a cloth bag made by Mary on her treadle sewing machine that was kindly donated by an old lady in Windrush village.

'You'll need it more than me,' she said. 'I'm a bit too arthritic now to use it.' She was right. It had been a godsend to Mary who could revamp old clothes for the family.

'What are we going to do, Daddy?' questioned Martha for the umpteenth time.

'I've told you and told you, lass. We're going to pick berries.'

'Why, Daddy?'

'We can take them to Whitby to be sold, Martha, and we'll have the pennies to buy food with,' answered Mary.

'Will I get some pennies for picking them, Mammy?' continued Martha.

'We'll see, love.' It was a new idea to Mary, this rosehip picking and she wasn't sure how much money could be made.

The little procession wandered along the pasture. Tom manoeuvred the pram up and down the bumps, over clods of earth and in cart wheel ruts. Mark seemed oblivious to his rocky ride, a very angel-faced baby with his rosy cheeks and beautiful, brown eyes. When he smiled, two dimples appeared in his fat, little cheeks.

'Dada, Dada,' he gurgled, as he bounced up and down and gazed around with great curiosity.

'Here's a good bush,' said Tom. 'Ready and ripe they are, Mary.' Tom parked the pram against a slight incline and lodged a grassy clod behind the front wheels to prevent the pram free-wheeling. Mary propped Mark up against his cushions so that he could watch what was going on.

'Good boy,' she said, as she bent down to kiss him, and added, 'lovely, baby Mark.' He smiled and gurgled,

'Dada,' yet again.

'When will he say anything else, Mammy?' asked Martha.

'Soon.'

'Come on,' called Tom. 'See who can pick most. We need lots and lots.'

Two hours later, the little procession wandered back home. They were all laden with bags of berries.

'I'll get down to Whitby next week, lass, eh?' stated Tom. 'Good job done, that. These will help a bit, as well as rabbits. We'll get by, lass. Don't worry.' Tom went to Whitby frequently for shopping and other errands. His favourite place was The Wellington public house. He downed many a quick pint in there or played a game of dominoes with his mates, or, in fact, with anyone who was available. Very friendly, charming and ready to talk, Tom made pleasant company. It was a welcome break from his hard work and worry at home. He enjoyed his trips out. He invariably went to the chemist shop and chatted up the assistants while making his purchases. The young ladies enjoyed the company of this tall, handsome man with his friendly smile, a ready joke and flattering comments. Tom would especially chat to blonde Margo and tell her all the latest news about his children. She too enjoyed the innocent flirtation. Usually, he took with him a large, laden basket when he went to Whitby to shop. After he sold its contents, he refilled it with purchases for home. As there were few buses each day, he planned his trips carefully to coincide with his farm work and times of the available buses.

There was a lot to pack for this trip. Mary placed the items in the basket most carefully. The rabbits were laid out neatly, their frozen, cold eyes staring out from stiff, fur-covered bodies. A dozen small eggs were packed in as the bantams were laying well at present, and finally there was a large bag, full of rosehips. 'Battery will do a bit longer,' said Mary, looking at the wireless, 'but the accumulator needs to go in.' It was a tricky business taking the accumulator, carefully balanced between Tom's feet whilst he was travelling on the bus. It was necessary to have it regularly recharged as the wireless was an essential part of their life. It was set up high in the kitchen on a small, wooden shelf, made by Tom, that, in turn, was fastened to the dark beams of the ceiling. The news and weather, Saturday Night Theatre and the boxing matches were highlights of a busy week. Workers Playtime was light relief at dinnertime. This way, the Holmes kept in touch with the outside world.

Martha wondered how the noise came out and where it came from. 'There must be a tiny little man behind those knobs,' she said to Emma, one day. 'He does talk and sing a lot, and mammy and daddy love to hear him.'
'I like the lady, too, when we listen with mammy,' added Emma. Martha pondered, screwing up her eyes as her imagination worked overtime.
'I suppose he must get tired, that little man. I wonder how he gets up there.' Tom overheard this conversation and was highly amused.
'Funny how their little minds work,' he said to Mary, late, one evening. 'It must seem a bit strange to a young lass, hearing a voice coming out of a box.' Mary nodded. She reckoned that life would be very dull without their wireless.

'Don't forget the mantles,' she shouted after him, as Tom set off up the back field. The mantles were for their new tilly lamps. They had two now. One hung from a hook in the ceiling casting a lovely glow around the kitchen. The other Tom took for his work outside. He hung it in the cowshed while milking and young Tim carried it around the buildings for him at night whilst he fed the animals. The only drawback was that the mantles kept getting holes in them making little yellow flames shoot out and then black patches appeared, dimming the glow of light. Still, it was progress and a great help to Tom when the dark, winter nights came along and he needed to move from building to building.

Mary was aware that Tom would be away for some time. An hour or two passed and she was humming away to herself when she heard a knock at the door. On opening it, she came face to face with Jack Netherfield.

'Morning, Mrs Holmes. I heard your little lass was in quite a bad accident. Thought I'd call by to see if she has made a good recovery,' he said, smiling at Mary.

'Well, you'd better come in then, Mr Netherfield.' Mary found him very attractive with his penetrating, deep blue eyes and with vibes of warmth emanating from his presence. 'I'll put the kettle on.'

'No, I'll do that,' said Jack, as he followed her into the kitchen, noting her slender figure with appealing curves, 'and please call me Jack.'

'Okay. Right. Thank you,' said Mary, a little flustered, conscious of her tattered apron and work clothes. 'You better call me Mary, then.' Jack pulled out his cigarettes and lit one for Mary and one for himself. Mary took two mugs down from the shelf. 'Take sugar, Jack?'

'No thanks and I bet you don't either. You know what they say, sweet enough without sugar,' he added, flatteringly. Mary blushed and turned to fetch the milk. It was a long time since anyone, apart from Tom, paid her such a personal compliment.

Tom, meanwhile, managed to find time for two pints of beer in The Wellington before catching the bus home. He'd sold all his products and was feeling pleased with himself. He was ready for a bite to eat.

'I'll have time before starting with milking,' he thought. As he turned towards the farmhouse, he saw an old, blue van parked outside. He did not recognise it as belonging to any of their friends, or the local dealers. 'Who on earth is visiting Mary while I'm out for day?' he wondered.

Tom's arms were aching as he reached the coals door. He was just about to put his basket down, when the door opened and he heard a voice say,
'And it's been grand for me too.' Tom met the eyes of Jack Netherfield, noticing that despite the warm smile on his face, his eyes were steely and icily cold. 'Well, hello there, Mr Holmes. We met at the sale, remember, and I've seen you at church. Just been telling Mary how much I've enjoyed the afternoon, but I'll be off now.' He turned and smiled once again to Mary who was still holding the door open. Tom watched him saunter off to his van and drive away.

'I'll take that,' said Mary, removing the accumulator from Tom and carrying it into the kitchen.
'What did he want?'
'He heard about Martha's accident and called in to see how she was doing. Kind of him, don't you think. It must be great having a van like that to get about in.'
'Well,' snarled Tom, 'he hasn't a wife and family to keep, has he,' disgruntled at his wife's obvious admiration for something he couldn't provide. 'He's a smarmy bugger, coming here while I'm out.'
'Oh, Tom, that's unreasonable, and you know I don't like you swearing in front of the children. Jack wasn't to know you'd be out. He was being neighbourly.' Mary couldn't understand Tom's antagonism towards Jack. He wasn't normally like this. 'Come on. Let's get this shopping put away and some tea on the go.' Tom said no more.
'Maybe it was all innocent on Mary's part,' Tom mused. This was the second time that Jack Netherfield happened to be passing while Tom was out and he was beginning to get a little suspicious of Jack's intentions.

Greener beyond the hill

1944

Spring arrived and with it, new life and activity after a bleak winter of hardship and poverty. On a bright, fresh morning when a blustery wind was whistling around the corners of the old farm buildings, Tom came striding into the house, his flat cap pulled well down his forehead, but with pleasure written all over his unshaven face. He called to his wife.

'Come on, lass. See what we've got. Bring bairns with you.' Mark was slumbering on and Emma was struggling to dress herself. 'Come down t' stable,' shouted Tom, as he disappeared again. Coats were quickly put on and woolly hats tied. Mary left Mark asleep and ushered Emma, Martha and Tim along the cobbles and into the stable. On the straw next to Daisy lay a newly born foal.

'Oh, Mammy. Oh, Daddy, isn't it lovely,' chorused the children, bright-eyed with wonder and staring solemnly at the foal.

The stable with its rough, brick walls, cobbled floor and the wind blowing in through the cracks in the door, was home to the two horses, Drummer and Daisy, plus Trigger the sheepdog, and the two cats, Smokey and Ginger. Now there was another occupant. As the children watched, the foal slowly struggled to its feet, its long, spindly legs splayed out to support the precariously balanced body. It turned its head and began hunting for milk. The children were fascinated.

'What will we call it, Daddy?' asked Tim. Tom pondered. He felt a great pride inside him as he stood stroking Daisy's side.

'Is it a boy or a girl, Daddy?' questioned Martha.

'It's a girl,' Tom replied, smiling. Mary was thinking of an appropriate name for this newly born animal and in doing so, recalled the day before, when she was standing in the kitchen, washing the pots and looking through the window. She remembered seeing tiny buds on the tree in the garden.

'The blossom will soon be out and everything will be pretty,' she'd thought. 'What about Blossom for a name, Tom?'

'Aye, that'll do fine, lass. Blossom, it is. By, I'm glad about this.'

Later that day, taking his older children with him, Tom went over to Charlie's to see about a plough he wanted to borrow. He told Charlie about Blossom.

'Couple of cows due any day as well,' Tom said, elatedly. 'Grand for our bairns seeing things like this.'

'Come on in and have a cup of tea and bring bairns in to sit down,' said Dorothy, appearing on the scene. Dorothy was always the same, warm-hearted, homely and quiet, her pinny tied around her waist and a clip holding back her mousey-coloured hair. She took the children in. The men followed. Tom often thought that Dorothy could be company for Mary and he hoped that they might get out occasionally. After a pleasant half-hour, Tom made to go.

'Tell Mary that she can come over with her bairns anytime for a chat,' Dorothy said to Tom as he reached the door. Tom smiled his thanks.

'I'll do that,' he replied. He was pleased. At least he could tell Mary that Dorothy invited her to visit anytime she wanted to. 'Maybe they'll start to get out a bit once they've met up a few times,' he thought. He knew Mary missed having adult conversation during the long days whilst he worked the land.

It was as if the whole world was coming alive. The grass started growing. The buds were sprouting and the children began playing on the pastures again. The cows were put out to graze during the day after being confined to the buildings all winter. A great mound of manure had built up outside the cowshed over the winter months. It was many days of hard work for Tom shovelling it into the cart, tipping it onto the fields and spreading it, before ploughing. Martha curled her nose up every time she walked past, as the smell rising from the rotting manure was putrid.

'It's a good healthy smell, that,' Tom assured her, jokingly. Martha was not convinced. Spring is a busy time for farmers. Tom worked from dawn till dusk, ploughing the fields and spreading fertiliser. Drummer and Daisy were a good team. As he yoked them up each morning, he felt a great pride and affection for them. Up and down the fields he walked behind the horses, following the plough or chain harrows and stopping occasionally for a cigarette. Sometimes Martha and Emma appeared, carrying a billycan of tea and with it, a sandwich.

Working on his fields, Tom could see Charlie on the far slopes, also preparing the land for sowing. The beck at the bottom of the pasture was the boundary line between their lands and there was an old, wooden railway sleeper placed across it so that Crossbeck farm could be reached more quickly than by following the longer cart track that wound around the fields. Tom frequently walked across the plank to reach Crossbeck when visiting Charlie and he pointed out to Tim this shorter route. Tom now worried about Martha and Emma crossing over the wooden plank when they went to play with Charlie's children. When Tim was with them, he was less anxious but when they were on their own, he was concerned that they might slip and end up in the running waters underneath. So far, they'd managed without difficulty. He noticed lately that the plank was a bit rotten in places.

'I must tell bairns not to use it any more,' he thought. 'I'll have to get rid of that plank.'

Tom's fears about his wife were not so easily pushed aside. Mary's health was slowly deteriorating as the winter progressed. She became nervy and edgy. She started shouting and sometimes even screaming at the children. He was glad that they could get out into the fresh air to play in freedom. He often took them to the fields with him to give his wife a break. It was during hay time that it became evident that it was a physical problem causing her distress. In past summers, Mary came with Tom to and help him to cock the hay and load the wagon, but this year she complained.

'I can't, Tom. My back's worse. You'll have to get help. Young Henry from Marsh farm might help you.' Henry came occasionally to give Tom a hand. Tom finally persuaded Mary to go and see the doctor.

'If you walk across to Charlie's, he'll take you to Shepton in his van.' Mary eventually made the arrangements when she saw Charlie at church. One Friday morning, Charlie came over, picked up Mary and drove her to the surgery at Shepton. He waited for her and brought her back home.

Tom was just pulling into the stack yard with a wagon load of hay when he saw Charlie's van pulling away from the house. Martha and Emma, in their cotton frocks, ran up to their mammy to say hello.

'They've been very good,' said Tom, rubbing his hand across his sweating brow. 'Put kettle on, lass, and we'll have a mug of tea. Henry here could do with one.' Henry was never sure what to say to the little girls and tended to keep his distance. He rarely spoke to Mary but was a good worker and was happy to earn himself some money helping Tom. The procession moved into the house,

Mary holding hands with the girls, Tom next and Henry bringing up the rear. Mary brought a few sweets, bought at the village shop, for Emma and Martha, a rare treat indeed. They scampered off outside free of their responsibility of minding Mark, who was sleeping soundly in his pram. Mary sighed as she poured out the tea realising that it would be much later before she could discuss her problem with Tom.

Many hours later, almost on midnight, Tom finally came in for the night. He pulled off his boots and tipped out all the hay and seeds that worked their way into them during the day. He sunk wearily into his old, wooden chair after a long day, but progress was made as half his hay crop was in. With a bit of luck in the weather tomorrow, he would get many more wagon loads. Henry promised to help again and his uncle Sam might turn up as he sometimes did on Saturdays. He would be a good help too.

'What's news, then, lass?' Tom asked Mary. She was gently rocking in her chair, her black, curly hair hanging around her tired face, and her eyes, looking even more deep-set, were emphasised by the black shadows underneath. She stopped rocking and sat up. 'I have to go into hospital. I've got a bad prolapse. My womb, you know. It needs surgery to put it back in place. Doctor wants to know if we're finished having a family. Seems to think I shouldn't have any more.' Tom's tired mind suddenly became alert.
'You mean sterilised?' Mary nodded.
'Doctor seemed to think we might need to discuss it. I told him we would.' Tom was stunned. He never thought that Mary might have to go into hospital. He sat there, unable to take in all that Mary said and the implications of it. He could hardly believe it. His mind was still churning over leading hay and milking cows. He realised that he was too tired to think with reason.
'Come on to bed, lass. I'm real tired. We'll discuss it tomorrow. You're not going into hospital straight away, are you?'
'A couple of weeks, probably when there's a bed. Doctor said he will do the operation, himself.'

They knelt, each leaning on a chair as they struggled to concentrate on their prayers which they said faithfully every night. Mary took the clock and wound it up before wearily climbing the stairs to check on the children. Tom went to pay a last call before going to their bed where it remained in the sitting room since Mark's birth.

Greener beyond the hill

He dropped his trousers concertina style onto the linoleum and crawled into bed. Mary, after putting on her nightdress, crept into bed beside him. They lay there, holding hands and trying to sleep, but both with thoughts that troubled their tired minds.

Mary and Tom spent days mulling over the decision. Mary received the letter with her appointment date. They decided against sterilisation. However, just after her arrival in hospital, Mary was called to the phone. It was Tom. He told her he had changed his mind saying that they should count their blessings. They already had four wonderful children. So why tempt fate.

'I must tell you, doctor,' Mary strained to say. She was ready in white cap and gown, and felt that she was drifting to and fro like a boat bobbing up and down on the waves. Her doctor was at her bedside with the sister-in-charge, and Mary wanted to tell him that Tom had changed his mind.
'All right, my dear. All right. Just relax and shut your eyes.' Mary could not get the words out as her mind slowly drifted and her body seemed to be light and moving.

Sorrowful though he was at the thought of no more children, Tom decided that it was perhaps best for Mary's health. He rode to Windrush village on Drummer and telephoned from the public kiosk, managing to have a word with Mary. However, because of Mary's sedated and muddled condition, the doctor misunderstood her and thought that she was trying to tell him not to do anything other than fix the prolapse. It was the next day that Mary started thinking rationally again and having discussed matters with her doctor, she found that nothing was done to prevent her having more children.
'You're a young, healthy woman,' the doctor told her, 'and although there is a risk, it doesn't necessarily mean that things won't go all right.' Mary thought that it was an act of God, that it must be that she was meant to have more babies eventually. With a further injection, Mary drifted back into a dreamless sleep.

Whilst Mary fretted and pined for her husband and children over the next week or so, especially for baby Mark, Tom was suffering at home. Early every morning, after hauling himself out of bed and dressing and feeding Mark, he gave strict instructions to Martha and Emma to look after Mark whilst he went to get the cows in. Trigger was quick at rounding them up and sometimes Emma went along to the cowshed to help give out the feed, at her dad's request, leaving Martha with Mark.

Emma was nervous and made her way very warily between two animals to tip the cow cake into the troughs. Each cow was given an allotted amount. Those due to calve, or having just calved, received more than the ones in mid-lactation or drying up. One cow did not get any, as she was not giving milk and should be *a bulling*, as Emma said. Farmers used this expression when cows were eager and ready for mating. Tom didn't own a bull and took his cows to a neighbouring farm to be serviced. Emma did not know the implications of this word but used the phrase because Tom used it. She wished she was bigger and braver like Tim as he was confident in chaining up the cows and would soon be able to milk an easy natured one. Emma did not think she would ever be able to sit on a stool, with a milking cap on her head, burying her head half under a cow, and squeezing milk out of it. Tom, normally very patient with his children, was decidedly impatient of late and Emma scampered off back to the house when she finished her chores, leaving Tom to battle on.

Tom kept going day after day doing the work of two parents. He struggled through the washing and fed the children with Martha's help, bathing and feeding Mark with clockwork regularity. Alongside milking and feeding the animals, cleaning out the pens, and collecting the eggs with a little help from Emma until Tim came home after school, Tom was extremely busy.

Towards the end of the second week, Mrs Williams, Henry's mam, walked down from Marsh farm and offered to do a day's baking. Mrs Williams was getting on in years, a hardworking woman. Tucking her wispy, greying hair behind her ears and with a wry smile on her face, she viewed the untidy kitchen, the unwashed pots and baskets of dirty nappies and washing.
'You little lasses can take Mark out for a walk and keep him out. Look after him while I sort your house out. Go on, off you go.'
'We've tried, you know. We wash up sometimes and get our own teas,' said Martha. Emma stood next to her, nodding vigorously.

Greener beyond the hill

A few hours later, Tom came in to a sparkling, clean kitchen with trays in the pantry full of pastries and cakes. The pulley lines were laden with dry, folded nappies and clothes.

'Oh, that's a grand bit of help,' he said, in appreciation. He was most grateful to Mrs Williams. 'What a difference a woman's hand makes,' he thought.

Another day or two went by and Emma was feeling most unhappy. 'I wish mammy would come home,' she thought. 'Daddy doesn't sing anymore and Mark cries a lot and daddy doesn't stay in the house all day like mammy. I do wish she would come home.' She repeated her thoughts to Martha. As the words came tumbling out, little tears started rolling down her cheeks. She rubbed them away with the back of her hand. Martha carried Mark outside to find Tom to tell him of Emma's distress. He was in the cowshed, swilling out the remaining bits of muck with buckets of water and brushing down the cobbles.

'What's up, lass?'

'It's Emma. She's crying,' said Martha, struggling to hold Mark as he wriggled to get down. Tom sighed. He finished his sweeping. He took Mark from Martha.

'Put buckets away, lass, and then we'll have breakfast.'

He carried Mark past the buildings and went in through the pigs door to the wash house, now renamed by Mary as the back kitchen. As he approached the kitchen, he could hear someone talking. He walked in, slowly and quietly.

'Please God, bring my mammy back,' Emma prayed, kneeling and leaning on her mammy's chair. 'Please God, hear me.' Tom blinked and swallowed. He put Mark down and picked up Emma who was all watery-eyed.

'It won't be long now, lass,' he reassured her. He felt quite moved by her plea and it seemed her prayers were answered. A letter arrived later that morning asking Tom to meet the two-twenty bus that afternoon. When he told the girls, Emma began jumping up and down on the concrete floor with glee and Mark started laughing at her.

'Lovely. Lovely. Lovely,' shouted Emma. 'Won't Tim be pleased when he comes home tonight from school.'

Some hours later the whole family was reunited. The children were delighted to see Mary. The girls could not leave her alone. Mary hugged and hugged them. She picked up Mark and smothered him with kisses. She'd missed them intensely. Tom was very relieved that Mary was home.

A day or two later, one of Tom's cows was in difficulty and Tom needed a syringe. He knew Charlie owned one and asked Martha to go over to Charlie's to collect it. Tim used to do Tom's errands but with him at school, it fell to Martha to go. Tom thought she was old enough now that she was five. Emma was minding Mark for Mary. Martha went alone.
'Make sure you come straight home,' was Tom's last instruction. 'I'll be in cowshed.'

Martha knew she should not go over the wooden sleeper as Tom had told them not to, but she could not be bothered to walk the long way around on the cart track. She waited until Tom went through to the back of the buildings before scampering down the pasture and disappearing into the valley bottom out of sight. Reaching the beck edge, she could see the muddy waters with foam at the edges of the bank and could hear the gurgling noises under the bridge. She was a little hesitant before gingerly stepping onto the wooden plank. Inch by inch, she shuffled forward. She heard creaking and suddenly there was a loud crack as the plank gave way beneath her. Flinging her arms out to save herself, she fell into the freezing waters.

The beck was quite full and the current was strong. Martha was tossed and turned, spluttering as she tried to grab overhanging branches or pull at boulders sticking out from the beck bed as the water swirled around them. She tried screaming but the noise of the running waters smothered her cries. The water carried her downstream, crossing the border onto Jack Netherfield's land. The last thing she remembered was feeling a sharp pain in her head before everything went black.

About half an hour after Martha left, Tom went into the house. 'Where's Martha with that syringe?' he asked Mary. 'I told her to bring it straight to me in cowshed.'

'She hasn't come back yet but I suppose she should be back by now, surely?' Mary hadn't been paying attention as to how long ago it was that Martha left.

'I'll go over to Charlie's,' said Tom. He was annoyed. 'She'll be playing with bairns more than likely. Knowing her, it'll be water fights with my syringe.' A few minutes later, Tom strode into Charlie's yard.

'Now then, Tom,' Charlie greeted him, quite pleased for the distraction from his work.

'Our Martha here? I sent her over to ask to borrow your syringe.'

'Not seen her. I'll ask Missus.' Charlie walked into the farmhouse and a few minutes later, reappeared with Dorothy. 'She's not been here, Tom,' Charlie informed him, having questioned Dorothy. Tom's face drained of colour. He felt panic rising in his chest. He could picture in his head the rotting plank.

'I'll have to find her, Charlie.'

'I'm right with you, Tom. Where should we start?'

'I never saw her on way here. We'd better walk down t' beck.'

The two men set off down the fields until they came to the makeshift crossing. One half of the plank was hanging over the side, the other half missing. Marks in the moss covering the rocks were clearly visible as if someone had been pulling at it. The two men didn't speak. Tom's heart sank into his stomach. He waded into the water. It was murky but he could make out the beck bed. Nothing there.

'She's maybe further downstream,' Charlie shouted, over the noise of the water. 'We'll take a side each.' Tom scrambled over some boulders and waded through the shallower parts to make his way across. They silently walked alongside the beck scrutinising the waters carefully, every bit of the way. They crossed over the fence adjoining Jack Netherfield's land. The beck widened further downstream and was bordered by sandy flats partially covered by the overhanging earth. Lying on the ground half in and half out of the water, Tom spotted the drenched and dirty body of a small child. Tom's chest tightened as he started to run.

Tom knelt beside his daughter. He gently lifted her from the water and turned her over. She was breathing but her legs were blue. There was a cut on her left temple with blood steadily trickling down her face. Charlie scrabbled across the beck and came rushing over.

'Must have knocked her head, on rocks,' he offered. Tom took off his jacket and wrapped it around Martha. He held her tightly to his body as they made their way back over the fields to Bankside farmhouse.

As they arrived, Martha began stirring.

'Thank God,' thought Tom. Mary screamed in horror on seeing the limp body of her bedraggled, bleeding, little daughter, convinced she was dead. 'It's all right,' reassured Tom. 'She needs a hot drink, warm bath and some dry clothes. I think we got there just in time.'

'What happened?' questioned Mary, taking her little girl into her arms. 'What happened?'

'She tried to cross that old railway sleeper and damn thing snapped. She was swept away wi' current, bashed her head on some rocks and was knocked out cold.'

'But you said you were taking it down,' Mary shouted, hysterically.

'Well I never got around to it, did I,' replied Tom, trying to keep calm.

'Never got around to it! Never got around to it! She could have been killed. What if she'd died and all you can say is you never got around to it!' Tom could feel the anger rising in him.

'Look,' he shouted, as he slammed the door shut after Charlie stepped inside, so angry he could feel the veins throbbing in his forehead, 'I never got around to it. I work day and night trying to keep this farm going. Don't bloody go on at me.'

Tom knew it was no excuse. He knew the children used the plank and that he should have moved it. He was angry with himself. He was blaming himself for the accident and he didn't need to hear it from anyone else. He got the tin bath from the back kitchen and placing it in the kitchen in front of the guarded fire, half filled it with water from the tap by the fire where the boiler was. Without speaking a word, he made another trip to the back kitchen for cold water to add to the hot whilst Mary stood in silence, rocking Martha backwards and forwards. Then, picking up his cap from the table and knowing that Martha would be fine, he nodded a thanks to Charlie and walked out, highly embarrassed at his outburst in front of Charlie. He needed time to calm down. Mary turned to Charlie who had been standing silently observing this not knowing quite what to say or do.

'Thanks for your help, Charlie.' He nodded and turned to leave.

'Oh, I'll drop the syringe by later,' he said, as an afterthought. Realising it was maybe not the right time to have said such a thing, he nodded again and left.

Mary knew she'd been unreasonable but she'd panicked. Tom was a good man and would do everything he could for his family. She helped Martha to undress as she was in a state of shock and could barely stand. Her teeth were chattering and her body shivering. Mary bathed her, put her in her clean warm clothes and after giving her a cup of warm milk, gently tucked her up with a blanket, on the sofa. Although worrying about the words exchanged with her husband, Mary knew Tom just needed to let off steam. She would apologise later and make it all right.

At intervals during the remainder of the morning, Mary checked on her daughter's progress. Martha slept on and off and Mary gave her more warm drinks. Tom came in at one point looking rather sheepish and Mary put her arms around him. They hugged in silence, reconciling their differences after their heated words to one another.

'Is she doing all right then?' Tom asked Mary, with concern in his voice.

'She's doing fine. I think she's suffering from shock and the after effects of being in the freezing water but I don't think it's anything serious to worry about,' reassured Mary. Tom went and peeped at his daughter before returning to his work.

Martha stayed on the sofa all day and by evening she was perking up.

'Get up for a short while, if you feel like it,' suggested Mary on seeing Martha sit up. Martha did so. She stayed up late into the evening until Tom came in after finishing his work. After his supper, he nursed Martha for a while before carrying her to bed.

'Thank God she's okay,' he voiced, very relieved, when returning downstairs. 'I guess she was pretty lucky.' Mary agreed.

'I think we've been very lucky,' she commented, quietly.

With some effort, Tom turned his mind to other matters during the next day, especially the ongoing shortage of money. He was always racking his brains trying to think of ways to make a little extra money especially for Christmas. A day later, he came up with a brain wave.

'This is a good one,' he thought. He shared his idea with Mary. He reasoned that if they kept geese and fattened them up, they could be sold at Christmas to private customers.

Soon enough there were half a dozen little yellow goslings waddling around the farmyard and swimming in the water trough near the orchard. Emma thought that they were lovely at first but as the autumn months passed by, the goslings grew into big, white geese with long necks and large beaks. Two black beady eyes peered out of each head. She was scared one day when the geese started to flap after her, sticking out their long necks and hissing very loudly. She ran and they followed. She struggled through the bars of the gate that joined the barn to the stable. It was a passageway through from the stack yard at the back, to the front of the buildings. Once through the gate, she turned around and watched. The geese stuck their long necks through the bars but they could not wriggle their fat bodies through like agile Emma. She vowed she would not go out to the back again until the geese were gone.

Martha started school in the September. Every morning, she and Tim set off together with their bait bags on their backs. Up the back field they went, across the moorland, down through the Mudhole, up the other side, across the rough track and the long mile walk to Windrush. It was the same trudge home. Martha found school days very tiring and came home quite exhausted. Many tears rolled down her chubby, red cheeks as she came in, cold and wet. Emma was most concerned and distressed to see her big sister in such a state.

Some good news in September was that the Home Guard meetings were no longer compulsory. Mary and Tom were both pleased about this and more so, in October, when members were told that they could keep all items of clothing, as Tom found the boots and greatcoat especially useful.

Greener beyond the hill

It was another hard winter, cold and bleak. Every day in winter, Martha and Tim wore their boots. After a few days of walking to and from school, angry red sores appeared just below their knees where the boot rims rubbed at their flesh.

'You poor, little things. Let's get some cow's relief on,' said Mary, reaching up into Tom's medicine cupboard for the very large tin of thick, yellow, greasy, paste-like substance. It was used on cows' sore teats and udders and was an excellent treatment for sores on legs. Mary plastered it on Martha and Tim's chaffed skin where the red weals appeared. This helped ease the pain. Just as she finished, Tom walked in. He stood and slapped his hands across his body and under his arms to warm himself up.

'By, but it's cold out there, lass.' The children joined in, mimicking their dad by swinging their arms to try and bring some warmth back into frozen fingers. As the warm blood rushed down to the tips, the tingling pain was almost as bad as the cold. Martha began crying again.

'It's tough for little lass,' Tom said, and turning to Emma, stated, 'come on, Emma. Give dad a hand with fothering up.'

'Yes, Daddy,' she replied, as she went to get her coat and boots, but her tummy was feeling very nervous.

'Them cows, again,' she thought. She knew that fothering meant feeding the cows and making sure they were settled down for the night.

A few minutes later, Emma opened the coals door to meet a blast of sharp air making her catch her breath. She went down into the cowshed where at least it was sheltered. The warmth from the animals' bodies made the atmosphere cosier. Tom came in and started untying the cows' chains as each animal needed to go out and have a drink at the pond. He'd been to break the ice on it, so that they could reach the water.

'Give them each a turnip, Emma, if you can manage that,' he instructed.

Emma went out through the back door of the cowshed. The wind was icy. She went over to the turnip heap and tried to loosen the turnips but the top ones were frozen together even though with a covering of straw to protect them. She pulled and tugged though her finger ends peeping out from holes in her gloves were hurting with the cold. She finally moved one turnip and two or three more rolled forward. She picked one up and staggered back to the cowshed. By this time, Tom had all the cows out and was putting down clean straw.

'Good lass,' Tom praised.

Tom went back out for some hay. With his fork stuck in a large pile, he heaved the hay onto his shoulder and turned to walk back to the shed. The wind almost lifted it off but with his head down and his back bent almost double, he thrust the hay into the wind and struggled on. Reaching the door, he pushed the whole load into the middle of the cowshed, turning and closing the door behind him. Now it was easier for Tom to share the hay out, a fork-full to each stall in the corner of the trough. Emma, struggling with a turnip, jump back as Tom nearly showered her with hay. The hay dust covered her woolly hat and face and she sneezed as it tickled her nose. More minutes passed and Tom returned with another load whilst Emma continued with the turnips.

The two cats crept in to wait for milking time and brushed their bodies against Tom's trouser legs, purring loudly. He finished forking the last of the hay from the floor to the stalls, before telling Emma to let the cows back in. Emma opened the door and swung it back. She held it whilst the cows streamed past. They knew their own stalls and they meekly walked up the shed until each found its place and then, head down, started munching the turnips and fresh hay. Tom went from one to another, chaining them up.

'You'll have to learn to chain them, lass. They won't hurt you. They're content to be back in.' Emma nodded, but inside she was trembling as she was not confident when helping with the animals.

It was almost dark when Tom and Emma made their way alongside the building to go in for tea. The air was bitterly cold and ice was forming over the mud holes along the pathway. How lovely it was to walk in to the cheery warmth of the coal fire burning and the glow of the tilly lamp hanging from the beam. It was a hard life this time of year for farmers everywhere.

Christmas was almost upon them.

'I think it's time to get those geese ready to take to Whitby,' said Tom to Mary one morning. 'Folks will be wanting them.' Mary agreed, although she was dreading the work ahead, plucking them, after Tom killed them. Tom caught the geese, one by one, cutting their necks with a sharp knife before stringing them up by their feet to the door snecks of the building at the back. When Emma went to have a look at them, their heavy bodies were cold and stiff. 'What happens now?' she asked Mary, in the kitchen.

'Come on, I'll show you.' Mary reached up for the old, tin bath hanging from the wall in the back kitchen, the same bath that she used to bath the children in. It was very cold in the back kitchen with the wind blowing in from under the doors. She carried the bath into the kitchen and placed it in front of the fire.

'What's that for, Mammy?' Martha asked. 'It's not bath time yet, is it?'

'We're going to pluck those geese.' Tom brought in one of the heavy geese and laid it in the bath. Its head, with beak open, dangled over one edge, the white feathers on its neck coloured red with caked blood. At the other end, its webbed feet stuck up like two stiff, flat kites. Mary reached for the sooty, black kettle from the coal fire and poured boiling water over the goose. As soon as the water ran off the feathers, Mary knelt on the mat and, leaning over the bath side, began pulling the feathers out.

'Can we help, Mammy?' asked Tim, eagerly.

'Yes, son, but be careful you don't scald yourself in the water.'

Soon, all the children were busy trying to help by pulling out feathers. Some feathers, especially the wing feathers, were too difficult for the children to manage but the soft, downy feathers were very easily rubbed or pulled from the bird's breast.

'Be careful not to tear the flesh as they won't sell as well,' Tom instructed the children. Tom took over when a bird was almost plucked. He took it from the bath and laid it on the table. It was part of his job to tidy the goose up and take the insides out.

'Ugh,' commented Martha as she watched him pull at its innards. 'So, that's what you meant, Mammy, when you said daddy would draw it. I thought you meant with a pencil and paper.' Tom grinned.

'I suppose it's because you draw innards out,' he commented.

Hours later, after interruptions for meals, six fine geese, each with a large slab of goose fat over their breast, lay side by side, on the kitchen table. A label was tied to one foot of each bird, so that Tom would get each goose to its correct customer in Whitby.

'Fine birds, those,' he said to Mary. 'Take some carrying, they will. Fetch a bob or two though. Now bairns are growing up a bit, we'll have to buy them one or two things you know, books and pencils and suchlike, for Christmas.' Mary nodded.

'I don't know how you are going to get them to Whitby, Tom. They weigh a ton.' Tom agreed. 'What you need,' Mary continued, 'is someone with a van. You know, like Jack Netherfield. In fact,' she thought, suddenly, 'he would do it for you, I'm sure.' Tom immediately felt uneasy at the mention of his name, never mind having to ask him a favour, but it would be a solution to the problem.

'I'll walk over after I've done milking tonight,' he said, reluctantly. He would much rather have asked Charlie but Charlie's van needed a repair job and Charlie was waiting for a new part with which to mend it.

It was very cold, but with a bright moon, when Tom set off to visit Jack Netherfield. He begrudged every step but knew it was necessary. A dog barked as he approached the farmhouse. He knocked on the door.

'Who is it?' Tom heard Jack call.

'Tom Holmes,' he shouted. Tom could hear stumbling and something fall over. Eventually the door opened. Jack Netherfield looked dishevelled and bleary-eyed, with what must have been three days of beard growing on his face.

'What do you want?' slurred Jack. His breath reeked of alcohol and he was clearly very drunk. Tom tried to hide his surprise. Those times when he saw Jack, either in church or in the Hunters Lodge, and that one time at Bankside, Jack was always smartly turned out. Tom never thought he'd see him in this state.

'Maybe it's not a good time,' Tom volunteered, turning to go.

'No, you'd better come in now you're here,' Jack mumbled.

Tom walked through the porch and into a large, bleak, stone-floored kitchen. There was a fire burning on the far side. The room was sparsely furnished. With a quick glance around the room, Tom noticed a couple of dilapidated chairs, a table with burn marks, sporting an open packet of cigarettes alongside an overflowing ashtray, and an old dresser, its only adornment, a faded photograph of an attractive young woman.

'Pretty, isn't she,' Jack began, 'but she isn't here anymore. Walked out on me, she did, some years ago, about this time of year.

Pregnant, she was, with my child, or so she said. Found out one day she'd been seeing another bloke. Him and her ran off together and I came back here as chance would have, getting this farm. I haven't anyone now. You're so damn lucky, with your beautiful young wife and those little bairns and you know what's worse, it's... it's... it's...' Jack stopped. He took another swig from his bottle. He didn't want Tom's pity. 'What did you come for, anyway?' he snapped.

'I wondered if you could take me into Whitby. It was Mary's idea,' he added. Jack sat with his head downcast. He could have told Tom a lot more but instead, he just nodded.

'Aye, I'll come over tomorrow.' Tom thanked him and made a quick exit.

Mary was waiting up for him when he arrived home. Tom stamped his feet to get some feeling back into them and hung up his cap and coat.

'Well? Will Jack take you, then?'

'Aye. He's a sad bloke, quite lonely I think. He was half cut, he was. Seems his wife ran off with another bloke, pregnant and all she was. Anyway, I'm off to bed. Coming?' With this, Tom sat down and took off his boots. Mary knew the conversation was over.

'Poor Jack,' she thought. 'How awful for him.'

Jack turned up on their doorstep next morning around ten o'clock, clean shaven and smart with no trace of the previous evening's drinking binge. He'd been thinking about the trip to Whitby.

'I was wondering,' he ventured, looking at Mary and Tom, 'if Mary might like to come instead of you, Tom? She could do her Christmas shopping. It'll be easier bringing it home in my van than on the bus.' Mary's heart danced with joy at the thought of a trip out, spending the money they'd make from the geese and with such a charming man to help. 'Well, what do you think?' Jack continued. Tom didn't like the idea but he'd seen Mary's face light up and didn't have the heart to refuse the offer. Reluctantly he nodded his head, knowing it would probably do her good.

'Would you like to, Mary?' Tom questioned, hoping she would decline.

'I would indeed,' she answered, emphatically. 'You can see to the children for a couple of hours, Tom, can't you,' she added, a statement more than a question. 'Won't be a minute,' she said to Jack, and not waiting for a further contribution from Tom, she disappeared into their bedroom. 'Just a quick dab of perfume and a touch of lipstick,' she thought, looking for her handbag.

Tom and Jack finished loading the van before she arrived outside with her shopping bags. Mary waved happily to Tom and the children standing at the coals door. Tom couldn't help feeling jealous of the distinguished-looking Jack Netherfield with his fancy van. He felt almost sick to the stomach when contemplating how Mary seemed to have taken a liking to him, especially now that Tom knew of Jack's high regard for his *beautiful, young wife*.

The next few hours passed very slowly for Tom. Anger started to build up inside him. It was nearly time for tea and they still weren't back.
'Where the hell are they?' he thought. 'They should be back by now. I don't like this. I should never have let her go with him.' All he could do was wait. The clicking of the clock loomed louder in his mind but the pointers seemed to move more slowly. Tom was becoming very anxious about Mary. He needed to get outside to start fothering the animals for the night, before milking time. His emotions were in turmoil, a mixture of anger and concern. He heard the van pull up outside. He didn't want to face Jack and make a scene and over-react in front of Mary. He heard her come in.

'I've had a great time, Tom. Took a bit longer than I thought, though,' was her greeting, whilst not really wanting to look him in the eye. She was feeling more than a little guilty at her lengthy absence. 'Hello, darlings,' she said to her children as she put her shopping bags down on the table. She picked up Mark and hugged him. 'Mammy loves you,' she uttered, kissing him. Tom could see she was animated. She looked alive, young and very pretty. Jack followed her in and placed more bags on the table.
'I'll be off then. Grand day, eh, Mary!' was his parting statement.
Mary nodded over Mark's head, as the toddler clung to her.
'Thanks, Jack. I've really enjoyed it.' Mary walked to the door and waved him off. 'I can tell that you want to get on, Tom,' she said, in a demure voice on re-entering the kitchen. Thanks for minding the children. I've enjoyed the trip out so much. It was very

unexpected. I'm glad you didn't mind.' What could Tom say to that. He put on his old coat and flat cap.

'Coming to help, Tim and Martha?' he asked his older children thinking that Emma would be more useful minding Mark for Mary. He walked out confused and disturbed. 'Was something going on,' he questioned himself, 'or was it just his imagination?'

Edna Hunneysett

1945 Winter, Spring, Summer

Mary was depressed all through January and couldn't seem to lift her spirits. The days were still very cold with long, dark evenings. She regretted ever agreeing to having those geese apart from the memorable day out that she'd so much enjoyed because of them. She relished in the memory of sinking into the plush, red velvet chair near the window in the lobby of the Grand Hotel on the sea front at Whitby, sitting with Jack, with all her shopping done. She never told Tom that it was idling the time away, being served afternoon tea in china cups, by ladies dressed in black with white frills, that made her and Jack late home.

Mary missed the luxury of her town life, or, she wondered, did it just seem luxurious in contrast to the bleak hardship of a working farm. She sighed as another feather floated down from the pulley. She was heartily sick of the feathers and try as she might to remove all traces of them, they still appeared on shelves, tables and chairs, and clothes. Each time she pulled an item of clothing down from the pulley above the kitchen fireside, a new scattering of feathers floated out across the kitchen. The clothes rods were always laden with washing, either wet or dry and airing, and the feathers seem to have found a resting place up there. It was a nightmare. She vowed never again to keep geese for selling. She was just sick of everything. It was weeks before the last of the feathers disappeared from her kitchen.

Over the next few weeks after the shopping episode, Tom constantly went back over that trip in his mind. He couldn't let go of it. February moved into March bringing with it no relief from the cold weather. Mary was looking worn and tired. She was very irritable. Tom was concerned about her. Many times, he found her in her rocking chair, when all around her the work was piling up. Pots needed washing; beds were left unmade and there was a mound of dirty clothes on the back kitchen floor. Mary seemed almost oblivious to her surroundings. The two older children were coping as best they could, getting themselves off to school in a morning and fending for themselves after school. Emma helped with Mark whilst Tom washed the clothes and generally tried to keep things ticking over. He found himself spending more and more time in the house working and trying to cajole Mary into action, than outside. He gently persuaded Mary that that she must eat a little as she had no appetite.

Tom tried to think of something that might stimulate her mentally. 'Maybe if we get a dictionary and a newspaper regularly, it will help, provided it has crosswords in,' he thought. 'Mary always loves doing crosswords. I could arrange for postman to bring a paper every day. I'll get her a cheap dictionary next time I'm in Whitby.' Mary lightened up a bit at this suggestion. Over the next few days, Tom carried out his plan. After that, it was a common sight for Tom to come in from milking and find Mary at the kitchen table. She shoved food and pots to one side to make a space for her dictionary, pen and paper and became engrossed in her crosswords. Her spirits gradually lightened and she began taking some interest in the home again.

One morning in spring, Tom hauled himself out of bed and sat on the edge, contemplating. He pulled open a curtain and peered out. It was a bright, fresh April morning. There was a touch of frost leaving a nip in the air making him pull on his overalls with speed. Mary woke up feeling quite nauseous. She realised she'd been feeling quite tired over the last few weeks even though much better mentally. She loved her daily paper and the crosswords.
'Oh, I can't be, surely,' she thought, 'but why not?' She shared her suspicions with Tom. They were both overjoyed, smiling to hide their unspoken fears that something might go wrong because of the operation but neither voicing their concerns.

'I think it's time you had a break, Mary, love,' Tom said to his wife as she walked back into the bedroom. 'You look tired, and you've had a rough winter. You could do with a rest. How about your sister Maureen up in Jedburgh? Would she put you up?' Mary thought about this. She hadn't been away from Moorbeck since they first set foot in it. She was quite fond of her older sister although she did not care for Maureen's husband, Stan. He always seemed self-centred and pompous. She liked Scotland and the border country,
'That would be lovely, Tom. I'll take Mark and Emma when Tim and Martha go back to school. That way, you'll not be left with too much to do.'

'Good idea, that,' said Tom. 'Be nice for our Emma. She's been a little treasure this winter, helping, as have the older ones, but I don't want them missing school. She'll mind Mark a bit for you as well.' Mary wrote to Maureen who immediately replied that she would be delighted to have Mary and her two younger children to stay.

A week or so later, Mary was busy packing.

'What's a holiday, Mammy?' asked Emma. She knew that when Tim and Martha spoke of holidays, it meant they just stayed off school and helped at home. Emma did not know of any other kind of holiday.

'We're going to stay with aunty Maureen and mammy will have a rest,' answered Mary, as she pushed clothes into a very tattered, brown suitcase with a broken fastener, the only suitcase they possessed. A worn, trouser belt held it together. Mary was thinking that hopefully a rest or, at least, a change of scenery might do her good even though she would miss Tom and the older children. She relied on him so much and was used to having him in and out all day. Emma was wearing new shoes specially bought for the trip to Scotland and was dancing around with excitement, unable to settle to anything. Every time she knocked an object with her feet, she brushed her shoes again so they remained clean and shiny for the holiday. She was very proud of her new shoes.

'See, Daddy, don't they look smart?' she said to Tom, who came in to see if they were ready.

'Oh, Mark, you're wet again. Oh, dear, you really are a little wet tail,' sighed Mary.

'Come on, lass. You'll miss bus,' urged Tom.

The case, and bag for sandwiches and drinks for the journey were laid in the cart. Tom lifted Emma up on to the clean, empty sacks. Mary, looking very smart in her new black trousers, hauled herself up. Tom handed Mark to her. Mark smiled at everyone. He was so bonny with his moonbeam face, dark brown eyes and two dimples and his mother doted on him. Ever since Mary's separation from Mark for the stay in hospital, she felt she couldn't make up to him enough for having left him. Mark, in his baby way, sensed this and was now very much a mammy's boy. Emma, too, realised this and felt left out at times. Sometimes, she wished her mammy would fuss her a bit more. However, the thrill and excitement of the unknown holiday was helping her to feel less sorry for herself. She was full of happy and loving feelings towards Mark.

After a bus journey to Whitby, the travelling Holmes family settled themselves in a railway carriage on the northbound train. They were going, moving. Emma's tummy turned over with nervous excitement. She found all the railway stations fascinating places. At each stop, she stood at the carriage window and pressed her face against the grimy pane of glass to see all the comings and goings, the people rushing here and there. Doors were slamming and whistles were blowing. Trains chugged in with a squeal of brakes as they came to a halt. She'd never seen such a commotion. 'Mammy. What a lot of people. Where do they all live?' she asked. Other travellers joined them in the carriage and Emma was rather shy with these strangers around. The whistle blew again. More doors were slammed. Emma's eyes shone like jewels. She turned and smiled at Mary and Mark. 'I like trains, Mammy. Do you?' Mary only half smiled. She was tired and feeling rather sick.

It seemed an endless journey with so many stops. She was weary of changing trains with her bag and case and Mark to carry, and Emma to watch. At one station, more and more passengers crowded onto the train. Some soldiers came into the carriage where Mary was sitting with her children and there were not enough seats.
'You stand, Emma,' instructed Mary and Emma obliged, reluctantly. After a while, Emma's legs began to ache and a kind soldier took her, saying,
'Come and sit on my knee, lassie.' He lifted her up and perched her on his lap. Emma sat there, stiff and nervous. She wished she was little like Mark so that she could cuddle up on her mammy's knee. She envied her little brother. She longed for the journey to end so that she could get off this strange man's knee. The soldier took out a bag of sweets and offered one to Emma. 'Go on, have one,' he encouraged, but Emma still hesitated and looked to Mary for permission. Mary nodded and smiled. Emma took one and whispered her thanks. 'Would your baby boy like one too?' asked the friendly soldier, dressed in khaki.
'Only if it's soft, please. He might choke on a hard one.' The young man assured her that they were only soft toffees. Mark took one gleefully and beamed at the donor. Mary unwrapped it for him

and dropped the paper into her bag. The children chewed contentedly.

At last, their train pulled into Jedburgh station, just over the border into Scotland. Mary stood up stiffly and put Mark down. She reached for her luggage. With Mark's hand and the bag in one hand, and the case in the other, she squeezed out of the carriage door, urging Emma to follow closely behind. Emma was terrified. She felt swamped by people around her. She took hold of her mammy's jacket so that she wouldn't get lost. As they streamed past the ticket collector, Mary searched anxiously hoping someone would be there to meet her.

'Mary, Mary,' she heard a familiar voice shout, and looking around, she spotted her sister. Dressed in a navy two-piece with smart, silk stockings and high heels, Maureen came forward.

Maureen was a little taller than Mary, but with slightly more pointed facial features, although with the same dark eyes and curly, black hair showing the odd sprinkle of grey. She was very attractive and talkative.

'Oh, Mary, how lovely to see you,' she cooed, a gentle lilt of Scottish tone in her voice. She lifted Mark up to kiss him. 'What a bonnie, wee laddie, and hello there, Emma,' she added. She bent down to kiss her too. Emma smiled coyly and gave a big sigh. She was tired. 'Never mind, lassie. We'll soon have you home and fed. What bonnie bairns you have, Mary.' Maureen chatted all the way to her home, a short walk away, holding Emma's hand and carrying the shabby case while Mary was content to listen as she carried the bag and Mark.

Later that evening, tucked up in bed in a strange room, Emma tossed restlessly from side to side. Eventually she fell asleep. She dreamt of moving trains and soldiers and crowds of people. Every so often, she jerked and flinched as her nervous system reacted to a very stressful day. Eventually deep sleep finally took over and when Mary came to bed, both her little ones were very peaceful.

A few days later, Mary was delighted to receive a letter from Tom. *Excuse pencil and short note as it is quarter past three and I am going to try and catch the post today.* Mary knew that the mail van delivered their letters mid-afternoon and at the same time,

collecting anything needing posting. *It is now ten past four so I've missed the post.* She knew he tried so hard.
'Poor Tom,' she thought. He went on about the farm and selling the lambs when they're ready and about money. *I needn't tell you we need the money we always do don't we but we get along.* He signed it *All my love Tom* and added nine kisses. Mam was silent as she folded up the letter and placed it in her handbag.

After receiving the letter, Mary became homesick for Tom. She missed him and her two older children more than she thought she would and began quietly pining to go home. After a week, she told Maureen that the short stay was the tonic she'd needed, that she felt rested, but that she was ready for home. Maureen persuaded her to stay a day or two longer after which Mary insisted that she return to Moorbeck. It was ten days after leaving that the same small party arrived back at Bankside farm.

When they returned, Emma didn't have much to relate to Martha. 'You must have done something, Emma. Tell me,' demanded Martha, pouting her lip. She was developing a real sulky pout when she became cross. She was cross now with Emma for not telling her about the holiday.
'Well,' said Emma, 'we went to this big place, me with cousin Helen, and Mark in a pram. There were lots of swings and slides and round-shaped things that you sit on and someone pushes them. Helen loved them all but I didn't go on any. I stayed with Mark 'cos he cried if I let go of the pram.'
'Didn't you do anything else?' asked Martha.
'We ate lots of currants. You see, when mammy went to lie down for a rest, I looked after Mark. I used to take him to aunty Maureen's kitchen to ask for currants for us. I told aunty Maureen that they kept Mark quiet. She gave us them in egg cups. She once said that she thought it was me who really wanted them.' Emma smiled to herself, knowingly. 'She was nice, aunty Maureen. I liked her.'

The summer that followed brought long, warm, sunny days when Martha, Emma, Tim and Mark spent hours playing among the white daises and coloured clover in the pastures. The cows grazed contentedly or tried to find shade from the heat of the sun in the afternoons, swishing their tails to swat the flies that settled on their

rumps. Occasionally, Mary took the children down the fields to the
beck. It was a cooler place to escape to, on a hot summer's day,
this low-lying ground beautifully sheltered by tall, overhanging
trees where the sunlight could barely filter through the thickly
clustered leaves. A very steep bank lay on the far side of the beck
and provided a shelter from any breeze. The water was quite cold
but shallow at this point with large boulders and smaller stones
lying in the stream bottom. Sometimes the water was so clear that
the gravel was visible on the water's bed and it was possible to see
a slippery eel or silver trout sliding away under the over-hanging
turf on the far side.

One very warm afternoon in July, Mary, taking her four children
with her, walked over the pastures to the beck at the bottom.
'Can we paddle today, Mammy?' asked Martha. She was quite
confident about going into the water despite her terrifying ordeal
when the plank snapped. The children loved to paddle in the beck.
'Yes, all right, then.' The little girls stripped to their knickers and
waded in and out of the water enjoying the feeling of wriggling
their toes on the sandy bottom and letting the water trickle over
their feet at the water's edge. 'Why don't you build a dam with
clay, Tim?' suggested Mary. She was brighter these days, since her
short break in Scotland. During the summer months, washing was
less of a burden because the clothes dried so quickly outside on the
washing lines, plus Mary was finding life much less arduous as the
children played out a lot. She was managing to fit work in around
doing her crosswords, and was enjoying spending more time with
the children.
'That's a good idea, Mammy. Come on, you girls. Help me,'
shouted Tim. They set to, gathering handfuls of clay and pebbles
to slowly build up a mound across the water.

Mary lay back on the grass with one hand on the small swell of her
stomach, thinking of her unborn child, as Mark crawled around
her.
'How blissful,' she thought, 'lying here with only the children's
voices in the background to break the stillness of the afternoon.
Utter contentment. How could she ever have thought that she
would never come to love Bankside?'

Mary dozed on and off lazily opening one eye at intervals to
reassure herself that Mark was not straying any distance but he

was fine, toddling around, not venturing far, fascinated by the tiny insects that scuttled among the blades of grass. The children made a dam across a narrow part of the beck. Tim pushed sticks through it to make holes. The water, building up on the other side, was rushing through the tunnels and dropping down into the stream again like a row of miniature waterfalls.

'Come and see, Mammy,' shouted Tim. Mary pulled herself up and wandered over.

'Tim, that really is very clever,' praised Mary.

'I helped too, Mammy,' said Martha, proudly.

Emma lost interest and was throwing pebbles into the water to watch them plop to the bottom, causing small sprays to shoot into the air. She was trying to see how high she could make the water splash.

'I'm getting hungry,' she said.

'Me, too,' shouted Martha.

'Okay. We'll have to go, then. It is time for tea. Put your clothes on,' said Mary, turning to make sure Mark was still around. He was crawling up the pasture side. She looked to see what the attraction was. Tom was coming from the direction of the farmhouse carrying a basket.

'Tom, how lovely,' she said, as he put the basket down at her feet. He put his arms around her and gave her a squeeze.

'I thought we'd have a bite out on such a nice day. Save you bothering when we get back.'

In the basket were packed hard-boiled eggs, bread and butter, a pot of jam, a piece of cheese, some cream crackers and some home-made rock buns. The children rushed up to him and gleefully noticed the contents of the basket.

'A picnic, a picnic,' they sang in chorus. Mary smiled tenderly at Tom, thinking how thoughtful he was. Such an unexpected pleasure.

'Will you come and see our dam, Daddy?' asked Tim.

'It looks good, lad. We'll eat first and then I'll have a proper look.' Tom also brought a can of tea, a bottle of water and cups. The whole family sat around to enjoy a meal in the open.

'No mess to clean up afterwards,' thought Mary, eyeing the bits of hard-boiled egg and crumbs from the rock buns scattered among the daisies. As they were sitting there eating, the cows wandered slowly towards them from further along the bank side trying to find a suitable place from where they could have a drink.

'They're looking very healthy, Mary,' said Tom, eyeing his stock up and down.

'Yes, love, they are,' she replied, gazing adoringly at their children. She laughed when she realised Tom's adoring gaze was elsewhere. 'You and your cows.' Tom lay back, put his hand in his overalls pocket and pulled out his woodbines.

'You know, lass, I think life's pretty good.' He drew on his cigarette. The wisps of smoke spiralled up to join the shafts of sunlight filtering through the tress. 'Life is good,' he thought, 'especially now that Mary seems much better.'

'I must have overdone it today,' thought Mary to herself, as she lay in bed that night. Mary felt extremely tired and was experiencing a dull ache around her back. She tried to sleep but couldn't. Although the sitting room was a temporary bedroom when Mark was born, Tom and Mary eventually returned the sitting room to its former state and were sleeping upstairs again. Crawling carefully out of bed so as not to waken Tom, Mary went down stairs to get an aspirin. 'The pain's getting worse,' she thought. She sat in the rocking chair and dozed. It was a warm night and she stayed there until morning. She kept coming to. She felt so alone with a terrible emptiness inside her, not of hunger, but an emotional, psychological emptiness.

'What's wrong with me?' she whispered to herself.

Mary looked down, feeling a wetness. She realised her waters were breaking. She also noticed her bloodstained nightdress. She was bleeding from inside. She got up to reach for a towel from the pulley.

'It's my baby,' she whimpered. 'Oh, my God, I'm losing my baby. Oh, God, please don't let me lose my baby.' The pains worsened and the bleeding became heavier. Mary didn't like to shout for Tom. 'What can he do anyway?' she thought. 'What can anyone do? There's no-one who can help me now. I'm all alone, just me and my baby. Don't die, baby,' she whispered. 'Please don't die.' Mary sat there rocking back and forth as tears rolled down her cheeks.

Mary eventually laid down on the clip mat with the towel under her. The cock was crowing and the dawn breaking, but for Mary

there was no light to console her. The pain eased and she lifted
from amongst the blood and water a perfectly formed, minute
body, a tiny scrap of humanity, around two inches long but
recognisable; a baby boy. She cradled the baby in the palm of her
hand. Tears poured down her face. Her grief was indescribable.
No-one else experienced this short-lived life. No-one would
understand her emptiness. She felt alone in the world, isolated and
bereft. She rocked herself to and fro, wailing, as she gazed at her
son.
'Oh, God! Oh, God!' she moaned. 'Help me.' After a while she
folded up the towel with the baby inside and cleaned herself up.
She sat with the bloody-stained towel on her knees and waited.

Tom eventually came downstairs. He started to speak and then
stopped in horror at the sight of the bloodied towel.
'I've lost our baby, Tom. I want you to take this towel and bury it
in the stack yard, a hidden corner somewhere. Don't open it. Just
bury it, please. Don't ask me anything. Just do it,' ordered Mary.
Tears were streaming down her cheeks and dripping on to her
nightdress. Tom took the towel carefully from her and went out.
He was back in half an hour. 'Now you'll have to ring the doctor
and tell him everything,' Mary said, gently. Tom was silent. He
went out a second time to carry out Mary's instructions, no
questions asked. He was back within the hour.
'Ambulance will be coming shortly. You won't be in hospital
long.' Mary said nothing. She cared about nothing. She was numb
with shock and grief.

The following day, Mary lay in hospital staring out of the window,
ignoring the hustle and bustle of visiting time. She knew that Tom
couldn't come because of the children and the farm. She was
surprised to see someone approaching her bed.
'I heard on the grapevine,' Jack Netherfield explained. 'Brought
you these.' He placed a large bunch of flowers on the bedside
table. Mary's eyes filled with tears. Jack reached out and took her
hand. 'I'm really sorry. I really am,' he ventured. 'Losing a child is
a terrible thing.'
'What a sensitive man,' thought Mary.
'When my lass walked out on me,' Jack continued, 'you could say
I lost my baby in a way. I loved that unborn baby.' His grip
tightened on Mary's fingers and he gazed intensely into her eyes as

if he was reading her soul. He leaned forward and gently placed his lips upon her cheek and held them there for a moment, both of then sharing each other's pain. Mary pulled away, conscious of their closeness. Jack stood up. 'I must go now. Take care,' he said, softly, and with that, he was gone.

When Mary returned home, she casually told Tom of Jack's visit. 'He's had a rough time of it, hasn't he,' she stated. Tom couldn't come to terms with Jack's interest in his wife. He was annoyed that he could not have been there to comfort Mary.
'I'd like to thump him,' he thought. 'I don't care if he's had a rough time. There's other women about. He should leave my lass alone. It's not right.' But Tom daren't voice these thoughts to Mary. She could see no harm in Jack. To her, he was a friend.

Greener beyond the hill

1945 Autumn

Autumn arrived and Emma began the daily trek to school with Tim and Martha. It was pig killing time for Tom. Mary knew that pig owners needed licences to keep pigs as well as having to complete forms declaring how many pigs they owned. Mary made sure that Tom's paper work was in order as inspectors from the Ministry regularly checked by visiting the premises. The number of pigs slaughtered was strictly licensed too but it was possible to obtain a licence to kill a pig and Tom's arrived a few days ago, thanks to Mary. He planned for a Saturday much to Emma's delight as she wanted to watch what happened.

Mary lit the copper fire in the back kitchen very early as the farmers needed plenty of water for scalding the pig. After he delivered the milk to the stand at the end of the cart track, Charlie arrived to help. Henry from Marsh farm was coming shortly to join them. Uncle Sam was also expected. Mary warned the children about the noise they would hear when they caught the pig to kill it but Emma did not want to hear the pig squealing and tried her hardest to blot out the noise by standing in the passageway, holding her hands tightly over her ears. The previous evening, Martha and Emma were fascinated to see Tom sharpen all his butchering knives. They watched him bring the tub and creel that he'd borrowed from a neighbour, into the back yard.

'Pigs are strange animals,' Martha thought. 'They seem to eat anything, even all that stuff that goes into the pig bucket.' The bucket stood in the back kitchen and all food waste went into it. Many times, Martha emptied the tea leaves from the teapot into it. Mary put in potato peelings and any leftovers that Trigger didn't want. Every bit of waste went into that bucket. When the bucket was full, Tom poured its contents into the pig troughs through the openings on the outside of their sty. Emma sometimes stood on the cobbles and peered into the troughs to watch the pigs as they sucked and chomped the rotten gunk. She remembered them with their flapping ears and round, fat, cumbersome, pink bodies, on short trotters, roaming the stack yard whilst Tom cleaned out their sty. Emma, quite frightened of their grunting and snorting as they rooted and heaved turfs and soil with their long snouts, watched them through the gate bars.

'Well, I'm going to see one of them dead,' she thought. 'I wonder if it's stopped squealing yet.'

'What's the matter, Emma,' questioned Mary, coming through the passage to the kitchen.
'I don't like that squealing, Mammy. Have they killed it yet?' At that moment, Tim walked in.
It's dead,' he informed them, matter-of-factly. Emma took her old coat from one of the nails behind the kitchen door, fastening the one button still intact, and put on her boots.
'Can I go and see, please, Mammy?'
'All right, Martha can mind Mark for me. Emma made her way through the back kitchen and out of the pigs door. The tub was standing on the cobbles and the pig was laid full stretch in it, its long body filling the whole of the tub. Tom came out carrying a milk bucket steaming with hot water.
'Stand well back, Emma,' he ordered. Tom poured the scalding water over the pig. He went in for another bucketful whilst Charlie, joined by Henry, began scraping the tough skin removing the short, stiff bristles that covered the pig's body. Uncle Sam, on arriving and greeting Mary, went immediately out to give a hand. Emma thought it strange to see this massive animal so still and quiet after having seen it so many times, ferocious and noisy.

Later, the men heaved the heavy body up on to the creel and began scraping again to remove the remaining bristles from the coarse flesh.
'It's a bit like what daddy does on a Saturday night ready for church on Sunday,' thought Emma, watching the men scraping the bristles, 'only daddy uses soap and makes a lovely white froth.'
She smiled to herself, as she recalled one night when she was standing a little too close to Tom as he stood in the kitchen shaving in front of the cracked mirror that hung by a piece of string from a nail in the wall. He was going over his stubble with his shaving brush building up a good frothy lather when he suddenly turned and gave Emma two dabs, one on each cheek. 'Oh, Daddy,' she squealed, before grabbing the towel to clean her face. Tom grinned.
'Some for you as well, Martha,' he said, swinging round and brushing her across the chin. He enjoyed a bit of teasing with his daughters.

Greener beyond the hill

Emma came back to the present with Mary's voice calling and she went in to help Martha with Mark. It was later before she could slip out again to see what progress was being made. The pig was hanging on a cambrill in the barn. Its back feet were outstretched and there was a deep cut down the length of its body. The men, having removed the intestines and liver, were washing the body down. Emma lost interest and wandered out of the barn and across the cobbles towards the house. Mary was shouting again.

Mary was feeling rough today and knew the reason why, as she realised a few days ago, that she was expecting another baby. She was overjoyed, having felt very unsettled after her miscarriage and although she knew this baby could never replace the one she lost, it may help to heal the psychological loss. Mary was not looking forward to her next chore spending hours cutting up the huge chunks of pig fat into small cubes. These she would render down, pouring the melted fat into huge seven-pound stone jars. The cubes of fat were stirred and put back into the oven for a further melt down. This process continued until all that remained were crisp scraps. It was an arduous task, done many times before but she could not get enthusiastic about it especially not today when she was feeling so nauseous. Mary balked at the sight of all that fat. Feeling so ill in a morning during these early weeks of pregnancy, she could retch over all these pieces of pig. It wasn't just the fat, but all the sorting of the liver and heart and other pig bits into packs for Tom to take to neighbours as it was customary for each farmer to deliver pig cuttings after a pig killing.

At some stage, Mary would make brawn but at present, her stomach seemed to come up into her mouth every time she thought about sorting off the fleshy meat from warm, boiled trotters and ears and other parts of the pig's anatomy. The massive sides and hams of the pig, after being cured in salt in the barn for three weeks were taken by Tom into the house and hung in the passage from the wooden beams. Pieces for cooking were easily cut from these, when needed. Mary was not yet accustomed to home-cured bacon as she found it very fatty and salty. She preferred bought, smoked bacon, a luxury, when they could afford it. The children loved the salty bacon, fried and put between two slices of bread and covered in brown sauce. Mary was so glad to have pig killing over with for another year.

Emma enjoyed her Saturdays at home as she found school days very tiring. It was a long trek over the moors and down the road to the village school and the Holmes children found it difficult to get there on time. The children already were accustomed to the walk because when Tom didn't take them to church, they went on foot. Sometimes a car pulled up when they were walking on the tarmac road, the driver recognising them, and they were offered a lift, but that happened infrequently. Emma told her mammy that she never understood why they sat near the front in church. Mary explained that in Saint Peter's, every family claimed their own bench. When a new family arrived, they used an available empty one. Tom and Mary chose a bench from the few remaining unclaimed. The children knew where to sit but were often late. Once, they arrived midway through the sermon. Everyone was quiet, apart from the priest with his booming voice echoing through the church, when the door squeaked open and the three children shuffled their way down the middle aisle, puffing and panting. Father Burnett stopped in mid track and waited.

'It was awful, Mammy,' Emma confided at the time. Martha was listening intently.

'We mean to set off earlier but it's so difficult,' Martha chipped in, 'with jobs to do beforehand. I dropped two eggs one morning because I was in such a hurry. Daddy was not pleased.'

It was the same trying to get to school on time. Mrs Featherstone, tired of latecomers, threatened to cane all those who arrived later than nine-fifteen. Emma was frightened of her teacher but she enjoyed writing, drawing and listening to stories. One morning, as an example, Mrs Featherstone, after many threats, caned five latecomers. There were a couple of children who lived in the village as well as the three Holmes children.

'Hold out your hand,' she instructed each child as they stepped through the classroom door. Emma received only one swish of the cane but she cried, feeling very upset as well as suffering the physical pain of smarting fingers.

'Others could help being late,' she thought. 'They don't have to walk all that way. How could anyone be so cruel as to hurt us when we don't deserve it.' She sat at her desk with her book open, unable to draw or write as her eyes kept brimming up and overflowing. She wished she was at home. She'd tried to hurry to school and her legs were so tired. Silent tears rolled down her cheeks and fell into wet blots on the paper.

Martha had issues too. One morning, it was still raining after
having poured down most of the night. The track through the
Mudhole was a bed of mud and water. Martha wore her boots as
did Tim and Emma, but Martha failed to tell Mary that she cut one
of them on a sharp nail, coming home the previous evening. By the
time she arrived at school, her foot was very wet, sloshing around
in water collected in the foot of her boot.
'Please Miss, my foot's wet,' she stammered to the teacher. Mrs
Featherstone tutted.
'You'd better tip the water outside and hang your sock on the
guard to dry.' Martha obeyed, hanging her wet sock over the heavy
guard that protected the children from the coal fire burning
brightly in the corner of the classroom. She stood her boot by her
desk and sat there swinging her bare foot feeling most embarrassed
at the dirty mark on her ankle, left by the water. Eventually she put
her sock back on, warm and dry, but the inside of her boot was wet
and the sock became damp again. Dinnertime could not come soon
enough. After Mrs Featherstone boiled the kettle on the fire,
Martha made a hot drink to warm herself, as she sat eating her
sandwiches. She longed for home time.

Going home had its problems too. When the Holmes children set
off walking with Charlie's children, the village children sometimes
walked part of the way with them and although this was pleasant,
Emma was frightened of Toby. He was one of Ben Edwards'
children and lived with his four brothers at Hunters Lodge, his dad
being its landlord. She knew that Toby was different to other
children as Tim talked about him at home because he'd plagued
Tim with questions when Tim started school. Toby was slightly
bow-legged and was developing into a tall, broad boy. He was a
gentle lad and never hurt anyone, but Emma didn't know this and
when he started chasing her, she ran even faster. Toby enjoyed this
fun.
'I'll get you. I'll get you,' he chanted and Emma's heart thudded
faster and faster until she felt it would burst as she tried to outrun
Toby up Beggar's bank.
'Come on, Emma. Run,' shouted cousin May.
'Toby, come back here,' yelled his older brother, Phil, with his
untidy, brown hair blowing across his face. Phil carried authority
where Toby was concerned. Toby turned around and made his way
back to Hunters Lodge. Emma, with the others, slowed down.

They walked leisurely the rest of the way home. Home, at last, with a tilly lamp for light and an outside toilet, cold and eerie in the torchlight. The cement floors were cold in their house and they used tin baths by the fire to wash in, but it was home, safe and comforting.

This year, the snow arrived early. Down fell the flakes, softly and silently, covering the tress and hedges so that they appeared to be shrouded in clouds. Excitement was building up in the kitchen at Bankside. Martha pleaded with Tom, yet again.
'Please, Daddy, aren't you going to get a tree?'
'Not until mammy says so,' replied Tom. 'All jobs need to be finished first.' The list of chores on Christmas Eve seemed never ending including the usual baking, washing the floors and shaking the mats. All the shoes were cleaned. Emma was longing for the evening so that she could hang up her sock for Father Christmas. Before that, she wanted to decorate the tree. She was most willing to help with any chore to speed things up. She tried very hard to amuse Mark so that Mary and Martha could finish the jobs whilst Tim helped Tom outside. At last Tom succumbed to his children's clamouring and said that he was going to the copse to cut a branch from the large holly tree. He wanted a branch big enough to stand in the corner of the sitting room. Although this room was a temporary bedroom when Mark was born, Tom and Mary eventually returned the sitting room to its former state. This room was used only on special occasions as it was expensive to have two fires burning fuel at the same time. Christmas was one of these special times.

As far as the eye could see, the world was a blanket of white. Tom trudged across the pasture, every step making a fresh imprint on the newly fallen snow. The branches of the trees that grew on the slope of the embankment and along the hollow at the bottom, were bending to the ground with the weight of the snow on them. The snow was falling continuously and everywhere around Tom, was still and quiet apart from the falling flakes.
'It is almost uncanny,' Tom thought, as he stood at the foot of the holly tree trying to decide which would be the most suitable branch to take. As he sawed through the wood, the snow from its branches showered him soaking through his coat. He was glad to be homeward bound, carrying the prickly, green holly with its clusters of red berries. Stamping his feet on the cobbles to shake

off the surplus snow, he came to the coals door and opened it to be greeted by smiling faces and shining eyes. 'You'll have to wait 'til all snow drops off,' Tom said to the children, as he stood the tree against the back kitchen wall. He left the dripping tree and went through to the kitchen to remove his wet coat.

'I see you've got box down from loft, son.'
'Yes, Daddy, mammy said I could,' replied Tim, feeling very big and proud of himself having been allowed to climb into the loft above the girls' bed to get down the square, wooden box that held their few but precious Christmas decorations. Martha loved the green bell that Tom was hanging up. It was very big, almost the length of her arm. It opened out and hung in the centre of the kitchen. She stood and gazed at it as it swung slowly this way and that.
'Oh, Daddy, I do love Christmas,' she said. Tom hung streamers across the beams. There was not room for many as the pulley washing line, with its four long wooden rods, took up a lot of ceiling space. Tom's shotgun was slung along one of the beams. A couple of small pieces of bacon, currently in use, were hanging from another beam and Tom needed to avoid the beam from which the tilly lamp hung.

During the last few weeks, Mary spent time painstakingly showing the children how to make Christmas decorations for the tree. Prior to this, she told them to save any brightly coloured sweet wrappers and Mary herself was very careful in saving eggshells from the eggs broken into two even halves, when baking. The children, under Mary's watchful gaze, stuck the coloured wrappers onto the shells. Emma found it very difficult as the shells broke so easily but Tim and Martha made some good ones. By the time each session was finished, the kitchen table was covered in bits of sticky paper and lots of broken eggshell. Emma ended up with paper stuck to her fingers but managed to make two decorations and was very pleased with herself. Later, when the children were in bed, Mary spent evenings carefully pricking each covered shell to make a small hole, through which she threaded a piece of cotton, knotting the thread ends together to make a loop ready for hanging.

Tom dragged the tree up the passage and into the sitting room. The children crowded around and it was soon covered with the treasured home-made baubles. Mark, two and a half, was a very determined young fellow and insisted on hanging something on the holly, but his dimpled cheeks were soon smothered in tears as he called out,

'I'm pricked. I'm pricked.'

'There, there, never mind,' said Mary, as she handed him a sweet, half unwrapped to give him the impression that he was unwrapping it himself. At last, everything was hung that could be. Tim, Martha and Emma stood admiring the cheerful tree.

'Isn't it lovely, Mammy,' said Martha, her face illuminated with pleasure and excitement. 'I can't wait for Christmas.'

It was still very early on Christmas morning when Tom struck a match and lit a candle at the side of Tim's bed. He gently shook his son.

'Do you still want to go, lad?' he whispered. Tim opened his eyes, his straight, black hair hanging over his face. He looked blank for a moment before he remembered what day it was. He nodded and slid out of bed, shivering with the cold air and quickly and quietly pulled on his trousers and jumper. Carrying his candle, he crept downstairs in his socks and opened the door leading into the kitchen. It was very cold. Tom was lighting the fire.

'I'll just have a quick look, Daddy,' said Tim, spying his sock with lumps and bulges in it. Lying under it was a new jumper and a construction set. By the time that Tim finished emptying his sock of its contents, the fire was burning brightly.

'Daddy, have you seen what Father Christmas brought me. They're smashing, aren't they,' Tim enthused. Tom nodded and smiled.

'Have a quick cup of tea and a bit of bread before you go. I'm off to do milking.'

Tim gulped down his drink after eating a hastily made sandwich. He pulled on his woolly hat and gloves. He was going 'shouting' for the very first time. Tom said that this year he could go, now that he was coming up to eight, and for past few days, Tim had spent time practising the rhyme. He was ready. Mary appeared in her nighty with her tatty, grey cardigan wrapped around her shoulders, a substitute for a bed jacket.

'You be careful now,' she warned Tim. She followed him to the coals door. It was freezing cold and pitch-black outside, not even a glimmer of moonlight. She called again as Tim almost stumbled on the cobbles, his only light being the weakening glow of his torch with the battery running low. 'Now be careful.' She watched his little figure slowly disappear.

Tim walked and stumbled across the track and up the bank along the lane to Marsh farm. There was no sign of life but taking his courage in both hands, he knocked hard on the outside door and then shouted as loud as possible.

I wish you a Merry Christmas and a Happy New Year.
Good luck to all you have, all through the year.
Big fat pig. New calf and cow.
Mister and Missus, how do you do.

He waited. Nothing happened. He hesitated, knocked again and repeated his verse. He waited. He heard noises and the door sneck rattled. The door opened slowly to reveal Mrs Williams dressed in long nightwear with an old coat draped round her shoulders. On her feet, she wore a flat pair of shoes with holes in the toes. She held a candle in her hand.
'Happy Christmas, lad. Come in. You're a plucky young 'un.' Tim stepped inside He could barely make out anything except a sink along the wall by the door. Coats hung on nails on the wall to his right. An assortment of boots lay in a jumbled heap on the floor. Mrs Williams walked slowly through another door. Tim waited hopefully. After what seemed a very long time, she reappeared and handed him some Christmas cake and a small piece of hard, yellow cheese. She pushed some money into his hand.
'Here, lad, take that.'
Oh, thank you and a happy Christmas to you all,' replied Tom, smiling. She smiled back. Tim was delighted with the money and went out of the door, closing it behind him.

As Tim went through the gate and back along the lane, he looked at the cake and cheese. He did not want the piece of cheese. He wasn't that hungry and it did not look very appetising at such an early hour. He wondered what he could do with it. He stumbled in and out of ruts and his foot caught in a deeper hole made in the soft earth by a horse's hoof. He has an idea. He pushed the cheese into the hole with his boot and trampled more snow and soil on it. 'Mustn't tell mammy,' he thought. 'She'd think I was being wasteful.' He placed the cake in his pocket, nibbling it as he made his way to Crossbeck farm.

It was a lengthy walk from Marsh farm. Charlie gave him a shilling. Tim crossed over the fields to Jack Netherfield's farm. By now he was tired and his legs were aching. It was hard work walking through the snow. He tentatively knocked on the door and chanted his rhyme. Jack was already up.
'Well, happy Christmas to you, young Tim. You've had a long walk. Come on in.' Tim walked in and warmed himself by the fire. 'This will warm you up, lad,' said Jack, handing him a mug of ginger beer. Tom gratefully took the mug and drank it in one long swig. He could feel the warmth creeping through his body. The heat from the fire enveloped him and suddenly he felt very sleepy. The excitement of the previous evening, the rising so early and the long walk were all beginning to tell on him. He forgot about getting home to help his daddy. He closed his eyes just for a moment. Jack looked across at him. Tim Holmes was sound asleep in Jack Netherfield's kitchen.

Jack sat and pondered for a moment watching Tim whose cheeks were glowing from the bitterly cold early morning air.
'Won't hurt the lad to have forty winks,' he thought. 'I'll look in on him later.' He knew that Tim should be getting home to help his dad. Jack took some twisted delight in thinking that this would annoy Tom, his son Tim, sleeping in Jack's home when he should be giving Tom a hand. Jack resented Tom having such a beautiful wife and a brood of children. It was not just his wife running off that made Jack so bitter. His hurt ran deeper than that but he couldn't tell anyone. Not yet, anyway. Maybe one day, when the time was right, he would confide in Mary and everything would be all right, but for now his secret would keep. 'I'll let lad have a good long sleep,' he thought, grinning wickedly to himself with satisfaction. He closed the door quietly behind Tim and went to do the milking.

'Hasn't he come back yet, Mary?' asked Tom, as he arrived in the kitchen with a bucket of milk to fill the milk jugs, for Mary. They always used fresh milk straight from the cows. 'He should have been back ages ago,' Tom added.

'You don't think anything has happened to him, do you?' questioned Mary, even more protective over her children since her miscarriage. She couldn't bear to lose another.

'No, he's a capable lad. I could have done with his help though. Little monkey. He's probably gone knocking on every door in Yorkshire,' Tom joked, but really he was quite annoyed. Tim knew that the jobs needed doing quickly this morning as the whole family was going to church. Tom told Mary and Martha that they would have to help while Emma minded Mark. The jobs were finished and everyone was getting ready for church when Tim arrived, over half an hour later.

'Where have you been?' Tom demanded, disappointed with Tim for letting him down.

'I called in at Mr Netherfield's farm,' Tim replied, looking very sheepish, 'but I fell asleep. Sorry, Dad.'

'Why didn't he wake you? You were needed here.' Tom was livid. 'Why is it that whenever trouble walks through my door, Jack Netherfield seems to be two steps behind,' he thought.

'He said he didn't like to wake me. He wouldn't know there were jobs to do.'

'Go and get ready for church and hurry,' ordered Tom. He was sceptical of Tim's last remark. He was sure Jack Netherfield, being a farmer himself, was aware that every pair of hands, children's as well, were needed to work the farm. Tom had this niggling feeling that Jack deliberately let Tim sleep, but he couldn't prove it and everyone else seemed to think Jack to be such a kind, genteel, neighbourly man.

'Come on, Tom. No time for day dreaming,' said Mary. 'We need to get a move on, you know.' Tom went out to hitch up the horse, astounded at the suggestion that he was idling time away. He was still fuming over Jack Netherfield.

1946

There were happy expected events to look forward to, during nineteen forty-six. Daisy was heavy with foal again. Tom loved his horses. He worked Drummer and Blossom as a team now that Daisy was due to foal shortly. Another was Tom and Mary's expected baby.

'Don't know which will be first, you or horse,' he said, jokingly, to Mary one morning, eyeing her enormous bulge. It seemed appropriate that spring should herald the births.

Mary was feeling remarkably well despite being like a barrel. Her sister, Maureen, was coming to visit and would hopefully be around for the baby's arrival. Mary knew she would be a great help to her and Tom.

'What's she like, Mammy?' asked Martha.

'Very chatty, friendly and gentle. You'll love her.' Mary was right. The children liked her very much. Aunty Maureen arrived wearing smart clothes and lots of make-up. She brought some almost empty, face cream jars, for Emma and Martha to play with. The jars smelt lovely. Martha decided than when she grew up she would put lots of creams on her face and be a beautiful lady.

Maureen brought some bananas with her for the family's tea.

'What are those, Mammy?' asked Martha. 'What do you do with them?'

'My goodness, Mary,' laughed Maureen. 'Have they never seen bananas before?' she asked, disbelievingly.

'No, they haven't,' answered Mary. 'You couldn't buy things like that during the war.' At tea-time, each member of the family ate a banana and later that evening, Emma felt quite ill.

'It's all the excitement, I suppose,' said Maureen. 'Come and sit on my knee.' Emma shook her head. She was very, very pale and was holding her stomach. Suddenly, she heaved and ran out of the house and vomited on the cobbles near the back drain. Time after time she heaved and spewed until her throat was sore. Maureen, who followed her out, took her by the hand and walked her back in. 'You poor, little thing,' she said, consolingly. She cleaned her up and took her to bed.

'Must have been those bananas, not being used to them,' said Mary later, lying back in her rocking chair, swaying gently backwards and forwards. Maureen nodded.

'I'm afraid it will be a while before Emma eats bananas again. You know, that bump's sitting on your knee. You look as if you'll burst at any time, Mary.' Mary laughed and patted the moving bulge. 'Another two or three weeks yet, the doctor says, although I don't feel I'll go much longer than a couple of days.' Mary was happy. It was lovely having her sister around.

The next day, with pinny on and ample advice from the two girls, Maureen cleaned up the house and washed all the dirty clothes she could find and hung them in the orchard. She worked briskly and efficiently and was quite able to cope with Mark and the others. All day she was watching Mary as they chatted. Every so often, Mary paused in what she was doing and glanced at the clock. As the day progressed, the pauses were more frequent during which, Mary clenched her fists until her knuckles turned white. Maureen realised that her sister was in slow labour. Maureen was a nurse and, although not experienced in seeing women in labour, knew enough to notice the early signs. After tea, she took the tin bath from the back kitchen and put it in the kitchen in front of the fire. 'It's not bath night, tonight,' thought Tim. He was growing tall like his daddy, with Mary's dark, deep-set eyes. He did not want this lady stripping and bathing him.

Maureen enjoyed washing Mark with his lovely chuckle when she tickled his rolls of fat. The girls bathed with no trouble. She dried them, rubbing vigorously with the towel.
'Come on, Tim. I've seen lots of little boys like you without clothes on.'
'I'm a big boy now and I can wash myself,' insisted Tim.
'Okay, then,' said Maureen and left him to it whilst she carried Mark up to bed followed by Emma and Martha.
'You are all beautiful,' she said, as one by one she kissed them goodnight. 'No talking now. Straight to sleep.'

By the time that she came down stairs, Tim was washed and wearing one of Tom's old shirts. He was kneeling by the fire saying his prayers. Maureen looked at Mary, questioningly.
'Yes, it's coming but it'll be some hours yet,' assured Mary. Tom with Maureen's help, again dismantled their bed and carried it downstairs to the sitting room. Maureen washed the linoleum-covered floor and lit the fire to air out the room. After Tom left the

room, she prepared the bed with guidance from Mary. Maureen was sleeping in Mark's bed with Mark sharing the double bed with Martha and Emma.

Much later, when Maureen was fast asleep, Tom came quietly upstairs with a torch in his hand.
'Wake up. Wake up,' he whispered. Maureen opened her eyes and tried to focus in the half light.
'All right, won't be a minute,' she replied, sleepily. Tom struck a match, lit a candle and went down again. Maureen joined him in the kitchen. It was three o'clock in the morning. Tom had not been to bed.
'Can you go across to Charlie's, please, Maureen. He'll drive to Windrush and phone doctor for me. He's already offered when time came. Mary's a bit frightened and wants me to stay with her.'
'Yes. Yes,' replied Maureen, putting on her coat. 'Can I have that torch, please?'

It was dark and very quiet. Maureen walked along the rough track. She imagined animals lurking behind the hedgerows and the slightest movement or sound sent shivers down her spine. She hurried on, following the little glow of torch light in front of her. Crossing the wooden bridge over the beck, she could hear the water running underneath. It sounded eerie. She brushed against an overhanging tree. Even more scared now, she quickened her pace. Everything was in darkness when she reached the farmhouse. She hammered on the door. After waiting some time, she heard noises and the sound of the key being turned in the lock. Charlie opened the door, bewildered at being disturbed by the untimely visitor.
'Quickly, can you go and telephone for the doctor, please? It's Mary.' Charlie grunted. He was still half asleep. He put on his big, grey overcoat, over his pyjamas, picked up his torch and walked down to the cart house to get his van, with Maureen following.

'It's on way, then?' he finally said to Maureen. 'Everything all right, is it?'
'Oh, yes. Yes,' she answered, briskly, wishing he would display a little speed. Charlie opened the cart house doors, got in his van, started the engine and backed it out. Maureen climbed in beside him to have a ride back, on his way out.
'By, look at that hedgehog,' Charlie said suddenly, coming to a halt and pointing to a prickly ball at the side of the track.'

'Never mind that. We want a doctor,' said Maureen, testily.
'Really,' she thought. 'Men. How can I get over to this farmer the urgency of the situation?' At the approach towards Bankside farmhouse, Charlie pulled up and Maureen got out, opening the gate for Charlie to continue driving, up the bank. After closing the gate, she made her way towards the farmhouse. Tom was waiting with a cup of tea for her. She took it into the sitting room and sat on the chair by the bed. 'Won't be long now,' she said, comfortingly, to Mary.

Tom was out milking the cows when Maureen ran to tell him the good news.
'A girl,' she shouted. 'It's a girl.' She tore back along the cobbles to the house. Doctor Mosey peered from under his bushy eyebrows at Maureen.
'Ever bathed a new-born baby?' he asked her, in his deep, gruff voice. She shook her head. 'Come on, then. We'll do this together.' Maureen was amazed and inspired by the manner with which he so tenderly bathed this newly born infant in the round, white bowl. His hands were deceptively nimble despite their huge size. The baby was long-limbed with a neat, perky face and dainty features. Mary lay back and watched. It was difficult for her to describe, even to Tom, the feeling of satisfaction and wonder mixed with elation and exhaustion after giving birth. She sighed and dozed off, knowing that with her sister around, all would be taken care of.

At first, Emma thought that her little sister, Amy, was lovely. As the weeks went by, she began secretly resenting her. Mary spent a lot of time bathing, feeding and cuddling this tiny child. Emma, when not at school, was told more and more often, to look after Mark. He was a boisterous, noisy, three-year old, who made lots of demands on his older sister. Emma sometimes was told to take Amy out in the pram, too, to quieten her.

One morning, whilst outside, trying to get Amy to sleep in the pram, Emma heard vehicles, not just one, but many, coming along the track into Moorbeck. Since the end of the war, Tom was continually badgering the War Office to improve the rough track that wound its way into Moorbeck because during the last year or so of the war, army tanks, driving in and out, churned up the stones and clay on the track leaving large holes and deep ruts everywhere. The tank drivers found the track leading up to the moorland behind Crossbeck farm, a good area for practising manoeuvres, as it was very steep and narrow and it had been a common sight to see them crawling up and over the top. The War Office agreed to have stone laid to repair the damaged track and the workmen, at long last, were coming to carry out the work.

Emma came running around the front of the house pushing Amy in the pram. In her haste, she misjudged the length of the shafts sticking out from the cart, parked on the mud flat outside the coals door. She ran full pelt into them. The impact brought the pram to a sudden halt. The jolt brought Emma's hands off the pram and it went up onto its hood, baby and blankets toppling into a heap inside the hood. Emma screamed in horror and Amy screamed in fright. The noises brought Mary running out of the house.
'What have you done?' she yelled. 'What have you done? Oh, you silly girl! You should be more careful!' she screeched at Emma, as she bent to rescue the baby and pull the pram upright. She cooed at Amy, and carried her off into the house, leaving Emma, standing there feeling guilty and ashamed.

Emma made her way around the back of the house and went into the orchard to an old tree trunk in the corner. Tom had cut the tree down for firewood and only the base remained, surrounded by bushes. It was a great place of escape. Emma sat there in the morning sunlight feeling miserable.
'Sometimes,' she thought, 'I get sick of looking after Mark, of washing up and then pushing Amy out in the pram.' Her self-pity welled up inside her until she could no longer contain it and tears sprang in her shining eyes until they spilled down her cheeks, falling on to her bare knees. She stayed there for quite some time until she heard a movement and saw Mary approaching.
'Come on, pet, you didn't mean to hurt Amy. She's fine now. Mammy shouldn't have shouted at you. You're such a good help to me.' Mary put a comforting arm around Emma who, snuggling up close, put her hand inside her mammy's and together they wandered down through the apple trees and gooseberry bushes, passing the duck trough and through the pigs door.

This same year, a Moors bus service began, taking in many small villages on its route. An early morning bus reached the turning to

Windrush, about ten to nine each morning. This was a godsend to the children who found the walk to school and back, tiring. One would have thought that nothing could have been better. However, because the Holmes children knew they could catch a bus to school on reaching the tarmac road, thus needing less time for their journey, they delayed their departure from home and repeatedly failed to arrive in time for the bus. Down through the Mudhole they regularly ran and up the other side, puffing and panting. 'Come on, Martha,' Tim encouraged, many a time, when she was a few yards behind, being a little less agile than the other two. Halfway across the heather and turf, they often spied the bus winding its way along the road. 'It's coming. It's coming,' Tim regularly shouted, being almost always ahead of the girls. Extra effort was put in by those six, tired, little legs as they sped across the moor. Invariably, the bus arrived at the road junction to Windrush before the children. The driver, quite used to waiting for them, held his transport for a few minutes until up the steps they came, gasping and breathless.

On other occasions, however, if he only saw little heads bobbing up and down in the far distance, he drove on, as he needed to keep to his timetable, within reason. The children watched the bus approach the turn.
'Will it stop and wait,' they thought. Their hearts sank when sometimes they watched it disappear, knowing that at the end of the long walk down the tarmac road, a scolding from the teacher awaited them, or even worse, the cane, for being late yet again.

Bonny, the foal, arrived shortly after Amy's birth and probably brought as much joy to Tom as Amy did to Mary.
'Well, not quite,' Tom assured his wife, but he had a lot of affection for his horses. He was proud of Daisy producing another fine foal. The children loved watching Bonny galloping across the pasture, throwing her hind legs into the air and tossing her head. Martha's favourite was old Drummer, though, as Tim sometimes led him to the coals door and allowed Martha to give him a crust to eat whilst she stroked his long, black, velvet nose.
'That foal doesn't take half as much looking after as Amy,' Mary mused, as she watched Bonny taking a drink from the pond.
Watching Bonny drinking reminded Mary that she must speak to Tom about the water. For days, she anxiously watched the flow of

water coming from the cold tap in the back kitchen, because it was
a much smaller stream than of late.
'I really must ask Tom to investigate it,' she thought.

Meanwhile she was scribbling a shopping list in time for the Home
and Col van, as Mary called it. This was something else new.
Since the track into Moorbeck was much improved, the Home and
Colonial Stores travelling shop began visiting the farms in the
valley. It came fortnightly and was a great boon to Mary. She was
careful to make a list of only the necessary food items needed as
she could not afford to indulge in luxuries. She heard the van pull
up and went out to get her shopping.

The driver, tall and lean, stood in the gangway of his van wearing
his long, brown overall, his head almost scraping the roof. With
his glasses perched on the bridge of his nose, he searched to find
the items that Mary read out from her list.
'You've a grand little family,' William said, as he watched Emma
and Martha scramble up the steps beside Mary, their dark, shining
hair gleaming in the sunlight. He spotted Mark outside the coals
door playing with his bricks and Amy asleep in her pram within
view of Mary.
'Yes, and I've got another, too. Tim is in fields helping his dad.
Got any Jacobs cream crackers, have you, and a bit of smoked
bacon, please?' William rummaged through his packed shelves
whilst the girls strained their necks to see what was on view.
'Are those chocolate biscuits, Mammy?' asked Martha, pointing
her finger in the direction of the boxes on a high shelf.
'Yes, love, but we can't afford them.' Mary responded,
emphatically. Martha sighed, thinking that there was never money
left for anything nice.

'Come on, jump down and let me carry your mam's groceries in,'
said William. 'That's three pounds, four shillings and six and a
half pence, Mrs Holmes. Will you check it, please?' he added,
handing her the bill. It was a lot of money. Mary had begun
asking, on occasions, if she could check the figures before paying
because once or twice she'd found mistakes after the van left.
Consequently, William always asked her now as he knew she
would check it anyway and he realised that Mary was
exceptionally good with figures.

'You're a penny out, William. I've double-checked it.' William accepted the correction and Mary wrote out a cheque. 'Go and open the bottom gate, Martha, please, for William.' Mary knew that he called at their farm on his way out of the valley, after visiting Dorothy's. William shut the back doors of his van and climbed into the driver's seat as Martha scampered along the cobbles. She raced along the mud track, now parched and dusty, and dragged the gate open. The driver waved as he went through, turning sharply to go up the bank. Martha waved and pulled the gate to, making sure it was fastened, before wandering back slowly in the warm sunshine to the house. There was a clear, blue sky with everywhere quiet and still, a beautiful day.

After putting all the groceries away, Mary went through to the back kitchen to fill the kettle but there was barely a trickle of water. Tom walked in, his shirt sleeves doubled up, exposing his hairy arms that were deeply suntanned. His shirt was open. He needed a mug of tea.
'Tom, look at this tap.' Tom watched.
'We'd better go and look at well in back field,' Tom replied, to Mary's insistence that he see to it straight away.
'Mind the baby, Martha,' called Mary. 'We won't be a minute.'
'Can I come?' asked Emma.'
'Yes, but bring Mark with you.' Emma and Mark followed Mary and Tom through the pigs door and past the duck trough, which was practically dry and through the stack yard leading to the back field.

A little way up the steep incline, partially hidden by overgrown grass, was a large, rectangular, metal lid. Tom heaved it up and peered in. Emma was amazed. She never thought about where water came from, but she could see that a pipe near the top, feeding the rainwater draining off the slopes into the well, was only just dripping. Two pipes fed the collected water from near the bottom of the well, underground to the house and buildings, but the deep well was practically dry.
'Not much there, lass,' commented Tom, closing the lid.
'What are we going to do, Tom?' asked Mary, anxiously
'We'll have to get some water from beck in churns for washing and just keep tap water for drinking.' They turned back towards the farmhouse with Emma skipping along beside them.

'Come on, Mark,' she encouraged, as Mark was dawdling.

After they ate, Tom went to halter Blossom and yoke her up to the cart. He put in two empty milk churns and a milk bucket. Tim, Martha and Emma climbed up too. They didn't want to miss the fun. Mary watched with Mark.

'There are always problems,' she thought. 'Fancy having to wash nappies and pots in beck water.' She sighed. It was a stifling hot afternoon and Mark was crabby. She could hear Amy's cries for her afternoon feed, coming from inside the house. 'Come on, son. I'll give you a drink of orange juice while the others are away.' She took Mark by the hand and went inside. A jug, strategically placed in the sink under the dripping cold water tap, was a quarter full. From the pantry, she reached for the bottle of thick, yellow, welfare orange juice and diluted a little. She stirred in a few grains of sugar for Mark to enjoy and handed it to him before going to pick up Amy.

Meanwhile, the older children were enjoying a bumpy ride until Tom pulled up where the pasture sloped steeply down to the beck, to let them climb out. He manoeuvred Blossom in and out of the bushes to reach the beck side and jumped down from the cart. Tim made his way on foot to the beck in case Tom needed his help, leaving Emma and Martha lying on the bank, the hot sun beating down on them. They watched in fascination as their daddy filled the churns with water.

'Our cows go and drink that, you know,' said Martha. Emma nodded.

'Shall we go and paddle?' Emma asked.

'No, it's too deep here and daddy wouldn't let us,' responded Martha, knowing full well that they'd be in trouble if they tried paddling. Emma turned onto her tummy and examined the blades of grass, pulling up a few daisies to make a daisy chain.

Eventually, Tom and Blossom passed by them going home with the water.

'You lasses can walk,' shouted Tom, and from the back of the cart, Tim waved and grinned. After reaching the house, Tom pulled Blossom to a halt outside the coals door. He untied the rope and lifted the churns down and bowled them into the back kitchen.

'I'll empty them in baths for you,' he shouted to Mary. 'Good job we got that new big bath.' It was a long, tin bath, much longer than

the previous one. Mary thought it was big improvement.
Sometimes she put it out on the front and bathed the children in the
cooler evening sun. The splashes over the side, ran away down the
cobbles. The children were much less restricted this way. It was
fun for them running around naked without a care in the world.
'After all,' thought Mary, 'who was there to see them? Only a few
farm animals and some birds!'

'You'll have to watch bairns don't fall in bath. I'll get some more
water tomorrow. Churns will need scalding for milk tonight,' Tom
called out to Mary, as he drained the last of the water from the
churns. Cupping his hands, he drank a mouthful of water and went
off to untie Blossom. The whole valley seemed to shimmer with
the heat of the sun. The cows, standing under the big, oak tree at
the end of the buildings, using what shade the overhanging
branches could provide, were swishing their long tails backwards
and forwards and up over their rumps as they tried to remove the
flies that clung to their skin to suck their blood. Sometimes a cow
began leaping about or running around, trying to shake off the
clinging insects. Tom licked his dry lips as he watched Blossom
trying to find some shade. 'Could do with a pint, myself,' he
thought. 'Maybe I'll get one later.' He met Martha and Emma
arriving back home from their walk up the pasture.
'Are you coming t' Bring and Buy sale next week, Daddy?' asked
Martha.
'Depends on weather, lass. Busy time now you know.'

Within days, Tom finished cutting the hay and decided he could
spare an afternoon to go to the church annual Bring and Buy sale.
The day before, Tom delivered Mary's homemade jam and three
cuddly teddy bears that she had painstakingly stitched and stuffed
during the drab winter months. On the day, itself, Mary made
cakes and was packing them ready to take.
'We'll put Amy in the pushchair and set off early, Tom,' Mary
stated, 'as soon as we've had dinner.' The children were excited
about their trip out. The night before, Emma cleaned all the shoes
and placed them neatly on the stairs, a pair on each step. She loved
dressing up in her best frock and cardigan. After she put them on,
Tom brushed her hair and tied it back with a clean ribbon. She was
ready to set off. 'Now, you help Mark to change,' said Mary to
Emma, 'while I feed Amy.' Emma was never sure which shoe

belonged to which foot and asked Mary, because otherwise, she invariably put them on the wrong way. Eventually, everyone was ready, Tom especially looking very spruced up in a clean, brown shirt and wearing his best trousers, his only trousers, instead of his working overalls.

Mary set off, pushing Amy. Tom, picking up the bag of cakes, followed with the other children.

'Will there be lots of ice cream, Daddy?' shouted Emma, as she skipped along by his side.

'Plenty enough for you, young lady,' Tom answered, with a grin.

'Getting tired, son?' he asked Mark, who nodded. Mark was sucking his thumb and dragging his feet. 'Come on, then. Up we go,' said Tom, as he swung Mark into the air and onto his shoulders, after passing the bag of cakes to Mary. Martha and Tim were walking in front, chattering like magpies.

'Have you got lots of pennies for us to spend, Daddy?' asked Emma. 'Tim says you can put your hand into a barrel of bran and get a present if you pay. Is that right?'

'Just wait until we get there, lass,' said Tom, tiring of Emma's incessant questions. 'Then you'll see.' He knew that in answering one question, another one would follow.

The family arrived to find the hall filling up. Mary handed her cakes in at the cake stall and made her way to the ice cream corner where she was a volunteer helper. She took Amy, still in the pushchair, with her. Tom was doorkeeper for the day and was also selling raffle tickets. Tim wandered off with Mark and Martha, leaving Emma standing beside Tom.

'Can I have some money, Daddy, please?' asked Emma. Nick Edwards, standing beside Tom, put his hand into his pocket and pulled out some coins.

'Hold out your hand, Emma,' he said. 'You're looking a very pretty young lady, today.' Emma beamed.

'Look, Daddy, two and sixpence,' said Emma, gleefully. 'Thank you, Mr Edwards,' she said, politely. Martha and Tim appeared with Mark and Amy. Nick gave all of them, except Amy, money to spend. Amy was sound asleep in her pushchair.

'You must be fair proud of them, Tom.' Tom nodded. The children spent money on the bran tub, roll-a-penny, and lots and lots of ice creams.

Towards the end of the afternoon, all the unsold goods were put on one table where there was a wheel of fortune. It spun round and round and the number at which the pointer eventually stopped, was called out. The person holding the ticket with the number on it, was the winner. Everyone was having a go and soon, all but one of the prizes were claimed.

'Just one large box of groceries left, to be won,' shouted Ben Edwards. 'Come and buy a ticket.' Emma was holding her last sticky sixpence in her warm, grubby hand. She bought two tickets for her money and could hardly contain herself waiting for the wheel to spin. 'All tickets gone. Round we go,' Ben shouted, spinning the wheel. Emma knew that her mammy and daddy would love that box of groceries and she longed to win it. 'Number seven. Who's got number seven?' Ben called. Emma looked at her ticket. She could not believe it. She was holding the winning ticket. She felt sick and her knees went weak. She nudged Mary. 'It's me. It's me,' she whispered.

'Oh, Emma. Go up to the front and show Mr Edwards.'

Emma was too shy to walk up and be the centre of attention in front of all these people. She half hid behind Mary, as everyone turned to look at her. A hand reached forward and took hold of hers.

'Come with me, Emma. I'll take you. You don't mind, Mary, do you?' Jack Netherfield asked. There were plenty of people around, listening.

'Not at all. Thank you, Jack. That's very kind of you,' Mary replied. Jack led Emma to the front to collect her prize and everyone cheered.

'Are you going to give me a tin?' asked Nick Edwards, teasingly. Emma only smiled. She was so nervous that she could feel her heart jumping inside her chest. She was happy, but it was all too much and she felt like crying. Jack carried the box under his arm as it was heavy for Emma and held Emma's hand with his other one. They wound their way back through the crowd.

As they approached the Holmes family, Jack overheard Tom saying,

'Mary, I've asked Jimmy Readman to take us home. Pushchair will fold up. Bairns are all tired.'

'I can take you all in my van, if you like,' Jack interrupted. 'It will be no trouble.' Jimmy, a retired farmer and almost bald, standing nearby, was listening to the conversation and chipped in.

'That 'll suit me fine, Jack, if you don't mind, as I've just been asked to do another trip. You'll be doing me a favour.'

'No, it will be my pleasure, Jimmy,' replied Jack, smiling. He was very pleased with this turn of events. 'Another chance to put Tom in the shade,' he thought.

'Okay with you, Tom?' Jimmy asked and without waiting for a reply, said, 'well that's settled, then. I'll be on my way.' He walked off.

'I'll go and put this in the van,' said Jack, still holding the box of groceries.

They all made their way outside and climbed into the van, clutching various prizes and sweets.

'We had a bloody good time 'til Jack Netherfield got involved,' thought Tom. He was seething. He was cramped in the back of the van with Tim, Martha, Emma, Mark, the pushchair and groceries. Mary sat in the front, nursing Amy on her knee, happily chatting to Jack. Tom felt Jack deliberately showed him up in front of his family and excluded him, by suggesting, as Tom was climbing into the front seat, that it was only gentlemanly to let Mary sit up front. Tom, like an embarrassed schoolboy, climbed down and crawled into the back of the van. Tom was beginning to hate this man. The truth of it was that Tom's male pride was hurt and he was jealous of Jack, with his van that was loved by all Tom's family.

Greener beyond the hill

1947

The snow was falling and had been for days. The cold, north wind
blew the snow in under the gap at the bottom of the coals door
leaving the snow lying on the cement floor like little, white
rivulets. It was very cold. The Holmes children did not return to
school in January because walking over the moors was, at first,
very difficult, eventually becoming impossible. Mary struggled to
keep on top of the washing. It was useless putting it outside, she
discovered, because when she tried hanging the nappies on the
outside line, they froze instantly and hung like stiff, white boards.
She found that bringing them in, hard and spiky, was also a
problem as they would not bend. They lay dripping whilst slowly
unfreezing, becoming once more, a pile of wet washing. Mary
hung the wet nappies and clothes on the pulley lines above the fire,
constantly turning them over and moving them along, and, as they
dried, removing them to make room for more wet items. The rising
steam filled the air with dampness.

Emma rubbed away the condensation on the window, and pressing
her nose against the glass, gazed out into the garden. It was
covered in snow like a big, white blanket. Large snowflakes began
splattering on the panes, blocking her view. She sighed.
'Give you a game of draughts,' said Martha.
'Okay,' replied Emma. Out came the board yet again. Tim was
reading, seated in Tom's chair whilst Mark was pulling a toy
tractor up and down the bumps on the clip mat. Amy was asleep in
the sitting room. The children heard the back door open and close.
Then there was a stamping of feet on the cement floor as Tom tried
to remove the remains of snow from his boots. He came through to
the kitchen, closing the door behind him and pushing the old coat
back in place at the bottom of the door to keep out the draught.
'I'll have a mug of tea before I do up,' he said to Mary. 'It's
getting worse. Never known such a bad year. Must go to Whitby
sometime soon to get more groceries as Home and Col won't be
up for a while.' Mary nodded. Throughout January, with the snow
falling continuously, the lane into Moorbeck was blocked. They
were marooned.

Up to the present, the farmers managed to get the milk out with
horses and cart, going through the Mudhole. The last few days,

this journey lasted hours with Tom and Charlie heaving and struggling to persuade the horses to keep going, before arriving at the road with cart and churns intact.

'We're going to take sledge tomorrow. Be easier than cart,' said Tom, supping his hot tea, his hands cupped around the mug to warm them. 'Coming to help to do up, you big 'uns?' he asked of the older children. They nodded and put away their games and books and went to get their boots. Martha and Emma rummaged through the hat drawer to find gloves without holes whilst Tim scrimmaged for a woollen hat. Going out of the coals door with their dad, the children were met with a gust of icy wind that almost took their breath away.

'You go and feed young calves, Martha and Tim, and give them some clean bedding. Emma, you come and help me wi' horses.' Emma followed Tom down the narrow channel that he'd dug out through the snow, with the snow now piled at each side as high as Emma.

'What a strange, white world,' she thought, as she walked carefully on the shiny, packed snow underfoot. The snow was drifting into great mounds around the buildings. Into the stable they went, pleased to be out of the gale force winds that blew down through the passageway gate, opening into the stack yard at the back of the house.

Tom untied Blossom's rope and handed it to Emma. She turned and led the big animal along the narrow dug out path through the snow to the pond where a little water lay low down under the ice, broken by Tom, earlier. Emma was full of trepidation, always fearful that the big hooves of the horse would come thrashing down on her as she walked slowly in front. After the horse drank to her fill, throwing back her head with the last gulp, Emma turned her round and made for the stable, not daring to run in case the horse did likewise, yet praying that she would get back safely to hand the horse over to Tom.

'Go on, lass. Tie her up,' said Tom, as Emma reached the stable door. In the darkened building, she walked up to Blossom's stall, fastened the rope to the ring and knotted it. With trembling knees, she sidled out close to the wall to keep well away from the heavy hooves.

'Can I go and help mammy with Mark and Amy now?' she asked, nervously, dreadfully worried in case Tom asked her to take Bonny out who, unlike Blossom, was quite frisky.
'Aye, go on, then. Martha 'll do others for me.' Emma's feet were already numb and her hands were pinging with pain as she made her way back along the narrow tunnel and in through the coals door.

The next day was a little brighter. The snow stopped falling.
'I'm off to Netherfield's, lass. Don't know what time I'll be back,' Tom said to Mary. He was wearing his boots and heavy overcoat, having changed his milking cap for his good church one. 'Tarra,' he shouted, from the coals door. He was going to walk across the field to Jack's farm as Jack offered him this lift when he saw Tom at church the previous Sunday.
'I'll take you to Keith Slate's funeral,' he'd said, and Tom didn't want to seem churlish and refuse an offer, just because he disliked the bloke. Mary was there at the time and encouraged Tom to accept the lift. He did so only out of respect for the deceased farmer. They arranged that Tom would walk to Jack's farm and from there, Jack would take him in his van. The funeral was being held in Whitby, as Mr Slate, a respected local farmer, retired there.

It was a long, hard, trek for Tom as he felt his way gingerly through the snow, sometimes stepping into drifts up to his waist. Eventually he was stamping his way across the yard at Jack's place.
'Thought you'd never get here,' was the greeting. Jack already was running the engine, to warm up the van. Tom climbed in and they set off. Tom lit a cigarette. He felt very uneasy with Jack. Jack was concentrating on driving. With much skidding and sliding, the van chugged its way up the track and onto the minor road that led to the main road. On reaching the main road, Jack took the right-hand turn in the direction of Whitby. There was no conversation between the men. The atmosphere was tense. The skies were darkening again and the wind was rising.
'By, it looks bad,' said Tom, at last, when the silence became too uncomfortable. Thick, white flakes were coming down, faster and more densely. Visibility was reduced to yards. The road was difficult to find because of the huge drifts, some almost the width of the road, that were increasing as the snow fell. The van

zigzagged along as Jack tried to manoeuvre it around the drifts. Rising in front of them were abandoned cars, looking like huge, snow piles as they stood, completely covered. The van skidded and ground to a halt.

Tom climbed out, and, dragging the spade from the back, began digging the snow to free the front wheels. Jack revved and revved and eventually the van moved. Tom climbed back in. Jack battled on but after three more stops, and with snowflakes saturating the air and obliterating any view, the men decided to abandon the van. They pushed it into the side as best they could and turned slowly round to walk back home. With their heads downwards facing the storm, they slipped and slithered along the bumpy road now very dangerous under foot because of the newly-lain snow covering the hard, packed surface of the frozen snow.

'At least, it's an excuse not to talk,' thought Tom, concentrating on his walking.

A mile or so back along their route, Tom and Jack came across a car straddling the road with two well-dressed men struggling to push it to the side.

'Want a hand?' shouted Tom.

'Yes, please, if you would be so kind,' answered the taller of the two. They all heaved and pushed. Eventually, the car rose onto a large bump, then sliding forward into the side, lodged itself in a dip.

'Going far?' asked Tom.

'We were going to Whitby to a funeral,' replied the taller one again. 'A relative of ours. We would never have set off if we'd known how bad conditions were on this road. We're a bit stranded now.'

'Keith Slate's funeral?' questioned Tom.

'Yes, that's right,' the gentleman replied.

'Like us, then,' answered Tom. 'Well, there no way you'll get back home today. Better come down to our spot. You can warm up and eat, stay the night and make an early start in morning. You'll probably get back t' town once you get t' coast.' Tom's spirits lifted. He didn't feel so strained now that they were with company.

'That's very kind of you. I'm Edmund,' the taller of the two informed them.'

'Dennis,' the other one offered, as snow fell from his ginger beard. 'Very grateful, we are.' Edmund nodded and the four set off walking. Conversation was limited as they picked their way over the snow, shoulders forward and heads bent facing another blizzard. A little later, Jack parted company to take the road leading to his farm. It was slow going as Tom painstakingly showed his companions the best places to walk, avoiding the deep drifts.

Much later, tired, cold and hungry, the three weary travellers arrived at Bankside where the warm, glowing fire was a wonderful sight. Hot mugs of tea with bacon sandwiches were gratefully received. Mary and Tom were delightful to sit and chat and hear about events in Middlesbrough where these two fellows, Dennis and Edmund, came from. The children charmed them with chatter and laughter. Edmund, taller than his companion and quietly spoken, clean shaven and fair-haired, told them about his three children and being used to youngsters, enjoyed the company of these little ones. Dennis, a jovial ginger-haired bloke, with a straggly beard, was playing cards with Tim, Martha and Emma, knock-out whist being one of their favourite card games. He was having great fun.

'We can play proper whist, too,' stated Martha. 'We often play at night with mammy and daddy.'

'Wonderful hospitality,' the visitors kept saying. 'We won't forget this.' The same words were repeated next morning, after a cooked breakfast of eggs and home-cured bacon, before they left on their long walk back to civilisation.

Within days the weather deteriorated further. The snowdrift in the garden was so high, that at its peak, it almost reached the top of the little plum tree. It sloped down to the outside ledge of the kitchen window. Tom left early with two horses, sledge and spades, to try and get the milk delivered. The milk lorry could no longer reach the milk stand leaving the farmers with no option but to take the churns to a pick-up point much closer to Whitby. It was essential that the milk was collected as it was the main source of income for the farmers in Moorbeck. They based their financial dealings around the monthly milk cheque. Late in the afternoon, Tom finally arrived home, tired but smiling.

'We made it, Mary, love, and guess what, among letters left in empty milk churns was a parcel for us. Very heavy, it is.' For the past weeks, the postman, unable to drive his van down into

Moorbeck to deliver the letters, was leaving them in an empty milk churn, knowing that this way, the farmers would get their mail. 'Open it, Mammy, open it,' chorused the children. This was excitement such as these children had not known for some time. 'What's in it? What's in it?' they kept asking. Mary pulled at the string and tore off the brown wrapping paper. It was a food parcel. She opened the letter lying on top.

> *'Dear Tom and Mary,'* she read, out loud. *I don't know if you'll remember me but I was the land girl who stayed with you not long after Emma was born. You were so kind to me and I loved helping with your children. Martha let me sleep in her bed whilst Tim made do with that tiny box room. It seems a long time ago now. I've since married and we have two little ones and we came to visit you but you'd moved. I did manage to get a forwarding address but never got around to writing until now. When I read about the awful conditions in your area, I thought I'd send you tins of food in case you are running short. Maybe one day we will come up North and visit.*

At this, Mary looked up at Martha grinning from ear to ear at the mention of her name. 'It's from Betty, Tom. You won't remember, children. Betty stayed with us in our other house for a while when you were very little. She was only young. She loved you all.' 'Well, fancy that,' said Tom. 'Grand lass, Betty. Must have read about us in papers. I'll have something to eat, Mary. I'll hear rest of news later.' Mary smiled. It was such a lovely surprise and good to know they weren't forgotten in this isolated valley of snow.

Tom was very disappointed over the next few days. He struggled to feed and fother his animals under appalling conditions. That, he could cope with, but for the last two days, the farmers were unable to get through at all with the milk and brought it back home. Empty milk churns stored for such an occasion, were standing full of milk in the back kitchen. It helped that, because some of the cows were producing little milk, having practically dried up as they were due to calve in spring, the yield was down this time of year.

'We'll have to fill baths, today, Mary,' said Tom. 'Can't afford to waste milk.' Down from the wall came the old, round, tin bath and

the long one. 'I can't sile milk straight in t' baths. I'll have to put it
in churns first,' explained Tom. 'I'll tip a half-full churn at a time
into a bath.' Milk was always sieved through cloth, into churns.
Emma was fascinated when first watching Tom empty his bucket
of milk, the rich, white stream flowing through the fine, mesh
cloth. At first, for sile cloths, Tom used cloth flour bags, after
Mary emptied them, opened the seams and washed them, but later,
he bought sile wads, made for this very purpose. The milk drained
through, leaving behind a frothy surface with hayseeds and bits of
dirt and dust that dropped into the bucket when the cows were
being milked. Soon the baths were full of milk from the churns.
'Might only be for a day or two,' said Tom. 'Tomorrow we can fill
up stone copper if necessary.'
'It's unbelievable,' thought Mary. 'I'm sick of the sight of milk.'

Apart from the worry and inconvenience of storing the milk, Mary
was not finding life too difficult, considering the circumstances.
There was plenty of home-cured bacon and as much milk as the
family needed. With the lard rendered down at pig killing and
stored in the big, stone pots and with flour from the large flour
sacks, she made pastry and bread. Mary, having bottled lots of
plums and gooseberries the previous autumn, was using the fruit to
make tasty pies. Although she had stocked up on tea and sugar,
this supply was beginning to run low, but the home-made jam was
lasting well. There were plenty of potatoes and turnips on hand
and the children seemed to be thriving on this limited diet. Weeks
passed by. The weather alternated between improving for a day or
two and then worsening for a few days. It seemed as if this pattern
would go on forever. Tom and Charlie managed to get the milk out
most days. They were very pleased that not one drop was wasted.
On the odd days when the journey was impossible, the milk was
stored and transported the next day.

Eventually, the snow showers ceased and the snow began melting
causing other problems, such as an early morning when Emma
found herself tossing about in bed wondering why she was awake.
She felt a drop of cold water on her face. Another drop hit her. She
opened her eyes and touched the pillow. It was wet. Still half
asleep, she rolled over, closer to Martha and snuggled down again.
She heard a plopping sound.

'That sounds like dripping hitting floor,' she thought, dreamily. Emma dozed off again but not for long. It was Martha who disturbed her this time. Martha woke up and finding Emma on her side, shoved her over.

'Get on your own side,' she said.

'I can't,' replied Emma, crossly. 'My pillow's wet.'

'Don't be daft. It can't be,' responded Martha, half asleep and very annoyed.

'Well, it is, Martha. It's dripping.'

'Dripping? What's dripping?' questioned Martha, irritably. It was lighter and the girls sat up in bed and looked around the room.

'Look,' said Emma, pointing to the ceiling. 'It's coming through there.' Martha turned her face upwards and gazed at the ceiling. Hanging along numbers of the brown, ceiling beams were lots and lots of little droplets of water. Martha was mesmerised. Suddenly, a droplet released itself and plopped onto her pillow. Martha could see that there were many damp patches on the bed. Emma looked over the side of the bed and noticed small pools of water on the floor. 'Come on,' she said to Martha. 'Let's go and tell mammy.' She crawled out of bed, pulled on her jumper over her nighty, and made her way downstairs.

'Mammy, Mammy,' she called, long before she arrived at the sitting room that was still being used as a bedroom since the arrival of Amy.

'What is it? What's the matter? Be quiet. You'll waken Amy,' said Mary, coming out of the sitting room.

'Mammy, it's raining in our bedroom, on my pillow and on bed and on floor,' said Emma, dramatically. Mary frowned. She noticed water on the kitchen floor and her eyes travelled upwards to the beamed ceiling.

'Oh, dear me. Oh, dear me. Tom, Tom, come here,' she shouted, forgetting herself that Amy was still asleep in their room. Tom wandered through in his shirt and bare feet.

'What's up?'

'Look,' said Mary, pointing to the ceiling. Rows of water droplets hung from the beams. Infrequently, a drop fell to the floor. From two of the beams, there was a steady drip of water.

'Loft must be full of snow. Blown in under tiles, I don't wonder,' said Tom, in his matter of fact way.

It was later in the day when Tom found time to go upstairs, followed by Mary and the children, to check out the loft. He moved the small covering from the hole and poked his head inside. 'Aye, there's loads of snow up there,' he stated to his listening family. Tom went to get a shovel and brought it, along with the round, tin bath that he put on the floor. 'Come on, lad,' he said to Tim. 'I'll put you up in loft and pass you the shovel.' It was a narrow opening into the loft with little head room inside. Tim started shovelling the snow out. The air was very cold and Tim was not enjoying himself. The rest of the family stood about watching.

'We'll have to get on t' agent. I think roof will need seeing to,' said Tom to Mary. 'We'll have to put all bairns in back bedroom and put buckets and bowls down to catch water.' Mary nodded. She learnt long ago to expect the unexpected, on a farm. 'I'll give you a hand wi' beds. What a going on.' He gazed out of the small bedroom window into the garden below. 'Another four inches visible,' he said, pointing to the little plum tree. Members of the Holmes family looked at the little tree regularly, to gauge the progress of the thaw as more of the tree was released each day from its white coffin.

It was wonderful that the long winter was finally coming to an end but it wasn't an end to their difficulties. Each night, Mary and Tom strategically placed buckets on the kitchen floor to catch the drips from the beams. Tell-tale signs were appearing along the beams where the water ran. Tim managed to get a lot of snow out of the loft but there was still some remaining that was melting and dripping through the ceilings. The children were excited about sharing one bedroom. There was chaos as they indulged in pillow fights and tussles that brought sharp reprimands from their parents, each morning.
'I'll be glad when they're back at school,' sighed Mary, after a particularly noisy start to the day. 'It's been a long, long winter.'

March finally arrived, in like a lion and staying that way. After numerous weeks of absenteeism, the children finally went back to school and for Mary and Tom, life returned to some sort of normality although there was still a lot of snow around.

Tim, having expressed a wish to be an altar server at church, was asked to attend a meeting, one Saturday morning.

'I really do want to go, Mammy,' he kept saying. 'I'll be all right. Daddy says so.' Anxious and worried for his safety, Mary thought it was crazy to allow him to go but Tom did not seem to mind.

'He's nine next month. Lad's growing up. He won't come to any harm.' After finishing milking, Tom yoked up Blossom and taking Tim with him, set off. Tim was growing fast and was confident in himself. He spent many hours digging snow and keeping the paths clear. He'd been on the milk round, numbers of times, and learnt a lot about trundling through the snow. Tom made his way to Windrush and dropped Tim off. 'Take good care, lad, coming home. I can't wait for you. Must get back to Drummer.' Tim smiled and waved his dad off.

Tom was soon home. Drummer was dying and wouldn't live much longer and Tom wanted to be with him at the end. Drummer was a much loved and trusted friend, having been with Tom through all the hard times. Tom's heart sank each time he approached the stable fearful that Drummer was already dead, but this time Drummer was brighter and seemed a bit more settled than of late. Tom went in for breakfast. He hung about waiting for Tim to return. 'Can't understand it. Lad should be back by now,' he said, after another hour passed by.

'You said he'd be all right. I wish I'd stuck out now. I didn't want him to go,' stated Mary. She was becoming very anxious.

Meanwhile, Tim, having come out of church after the meeting, began walking up the road through the village. A van pulled up and Jack Netherfield got out.

'Now, young Tim, how are you?' he asked.

'I'm fine, thank you,' Tim answered, politely. He hadn't forgotten the last encounter with Jack Netherfield and how annoyed his dad was at the time, when he'd fallen asleep in Mr Netherfield's house.

'Jump in, lad,' invited Mr Netherfield. Tim shook his head.

'Thank you, but I'd better be getting home. It's another half hour's walk yet.'

'Exactly,' said Jack, 'but I can save you that time. I'll take you home. Come on, lad.' He opened the door and ushered Tim inside the van. Tim didn't know how to refuse. In the van, with closer proximity to Mr Netherfield, Tim could smell his breath.

"It's like dad's when he's been drinking,' thought Tim. Jack's breath stunk of alcohol. Jack was grinning away to himself. He'd give that Tom something to worry about.

'He thinks he's got everything, he does,' thought Jack. 'Well, let's see how he copes with a real bit of worry.' Jack put his foot on the peddle and the van sped off.

'Where are we going?' asked Tim, a little scared of this man's manner.

'Oh, just for a ride. Maybe to Whitby. Who knows. Who cares,' laughed Jack. 'We'll just have a bit of fun, eh?'

Tim was frightened now. He sat in silence wondering what he could do he couldn't think of anything. He was glad that the roads were clear of snow although there was plenty piled up on the sides. Eventually they arrived at Whitby. Jack parked the car.

'Come on. Get out,' Jack said quite sharply to Tim. Tim climbed out.

'What can I do?' he thought. He followed Jack down the streets. They stopped at a bread shop.

'Want a bun?' he asked Tim.

'No, thank you.'

'Yes, you do. You can tell your dad what a kind bloke I am,' said Jack, grinning. He ushered Tim into the shop and bought two buns.

'There you are,' he said, giving one to Tim. They strolled along the pier eating buns. Tim did not dare do otherwise.

It was much later when they set off on their journey back to Moorbeck.

'I'll take you to the top of your last field,' said Jack. 'You'll only have the bank to go down. Saved you a lot of time me bringing you home, didn't it?' Jack guffawed at this last remark. 'Tell your dad I gave you a nice run out and brought you safely home,' he shouted, as Tim started running down the bank to the farmhouse. Jack was still chortling as he set off back to his own place.

'Where on earth have you been?' asked Mary, when Tim walked in. She looked at his eyes and could see that he was almost in tears. He started to tell her the tale when Tom walked in. 'Ssh! Ssh,' she went, raising her fingers to her lips. She did not want Tom to interrupt. Tom stood still and they both listened whilst Tim poured out his story.

123

'So, it wasn't my fault,' he finished with. Tom was absolutely lived.

'That man's not right,' he thought. 'I'll bloody kill him next time I see him,' he raged to himself. 'What does he think he's playing at?' It was days before Tom simmered down. 'But why?' he kept asking himself. 'Why is he doing this, or is it Tim's overactive imagination getting this out of all proportion? After all, he only took lad out for a ride, or did he?' he argued with himself. 'I'll have to have it out with him.' Every day, Tom's resolve to visit Jack was shelved because other needs were more pressing. He was too busy to find the time and the incident receded in his mind.

A few days later, Tom came in for breakfast, very quiet and sad-looking.

'He's gone,' he said to Mary.

'I'm sorry, love,' Mary said, comfortingly, as she put her arm around his shoulder. She knew he was referring to Drummer. 'He's been a good friend to you, hasn't he?'

'I'll have to get Charlie and Henry to help me dig a hole down at bottom of pasture where marshy bit is and bury him,' stated Tom. The snow was clearing rapidly in parts but was still piled up at the sides of the paths. The air was bitterly cold. Later in the day, Emma and Martha, well wrapped up in their old coats and woolly hats, watched the sad procession. The body of Drummer was roped to the sledge. Blossom and Bonny were slowly dragging the heavy weight across the pasture that was still splattered with snow. Tom and Charlie were at the front and leading the horses. Daisy, heavy with foal, followed behind.

The procession reached the steep part of the pasture and made its way to the marshy land at the bottom near the beck where a shallow grave was dug in readiness. The snow had melted more quickly here but the land was soft and dangerous. Daisy stayed at the top of the bank and whinnied.

'Think she knows her mate's gone?' asked Charlie.

'Aye, I shouldn't wonder,' answered Tom, his heart as heavy as lead, as he shovelled sods of earth over the body. Daisy turned and made her way back to the stable door.

Each day, when turned out for water, Daisy wandered to the top of the hill and whinnied. The sound was loud and clear. She was pining for her lost mate. It wasn't long before she joined him. Tom went on his milk round one morning after turning Daisy out. When he came back, he found her heaving and panting her last breaths, giving birth to a big, male foal.

'Another horse to bury and a pet foal to rear,' thought Tom, pensively.

'Little Drummer, we'll call him,' he said to Mary, when he told her of the latest addition. This, another pet to add to the string of pets they kept over the years.

'You can't feed a foal with a bottle like we did with the little pet pig, can you, Tom?' she questioned.

'No, lass, no,' laughed Tom, brightening up for a moment. 'We'll feed him from of a bucket outside pigs door. He won't be in house.'

'Thank goodness for that,' thought Mary, relieved. She was remembering the so-called fun with the pet pig. It used to run around and around the kitchen leaving little pools behind on the floor, much to Mary's disgust. Martha and Emma took turns, feeding it from a bottle with a baby's teat on it. The fat, little piglet dribbled and snuffled as it sucked down the milk at great speed. Umpteen times a day they seemed to be standing or kneeling in front of this squirming, little pink animal as it greedily guzzled down the milk. Mary did not think that feeding a foal outside from a bucket would be anything like the trouble the pig was. Tom, in his wisdom, passed no comment.

The snow disappeared and spring turned into summer. Emma and Martha were standing in the corner of the hay field, with Amy in the old, black pram, its hood falling apart. It was warm and the girls discarded their cardigans and deposited them in the pram, but no sooner had this been done than Amy picked them up and threw them out. Amy was growing to look like her sisters but with a more elfish chin and a little, pointed nose. The girls were watching Tom cutting the hay. The grass cutter made a whirring, clicking noise. Layers of cut hay in neat rows were drying out in the sunshine and the uncut patch became smaller and smaller as Tom made his way around and around the field.

'Look, Martha. A mouse,' shouted Emma, pointing to the scurrying field mouse as it scuttled between the short, cut stalks. The mouse disappeared as Mark came to join them with a can of tea and buttered scone for Tom.

'You're a clever lad,' said Martha, 'carrying that all by yourself.'
Mark beamed, showing both his dimples. He was as robust as ever
with short, sturdy arms and legs and an unruly mop of dark hair.
'Let's all wave to daddy to stop him,' said Emma. They waved
furiously. As Tom came up the side of the uncut grass, he glanced
over to the little group and grinned. He waved back to them and
brought the horse to a halt. Minutes later, he was sitting in the
hedgerow, drinking his tea and relaxing with a woodbine. He
pulled off his jacket and laid it under the hedge.
'By, it's getting warm,' he said, rolling up his shirt sleeves. 'Are
you taking can back to mammy, Mark?' Mark nodded.
'I'll walk with you, Mark, because I'm going back to help
mammy,' said Emma.
'I think I'll push Amy and go for a walk, Daddy,' said Martha.
Tom smiled. He wished he could spend more time with his
children instead of always working.

No sooner had the hot, summer days passed, that autumn set in.
The three eldest children were back at school leaving behind Mark,
now a hefty four-year old, and, in comparison, Amy, who was a
dainty one-year old.
'They are growing up,' Mary thought, waving for the umpteenth
time, as the older ones made their way up the back field.

The weeks passed by quickly. Soon enough it was Christmas Eve
and with it, all the hustle and bustle and last-minute preparations.
Emma, usually so vivacious and full of Christmas excitement, was
listless and quiet. Her lively face was sad. She mooched about
lethargically all day, not knowing what was wrong, but trying in
her helpful way to occupy Amy and Mark whilst Mary iced the
Christmas cake and finished the baking. After tea, Emma went to
bed early, followed a little later by Martha and Tim. They needed
to rest so as not to be too tired to go to midnight Mass. This was a
treat for the three older children. It added to the excitement of
Christmas.

Emma spent an age trying to fall asleep. No sooner had she
achieved this than Tom was shaking her awake again, or so it
seemed to Emma.
'Come on, time to be up,' Tom said to a very sleepy, little girl.
Emma opened her eyes, forgetting for a moment why she should
get up when she felt so tired. Tom woke Martha and left them his

126

torch so that they could dress by the beam of light instead of using a candle. Emma dragged herself out from under the warm blankets and, despite the chilly air of the cold bedroom, she dressed very slowly. Downstairs, Amy's tiny sock was sticking out of the fireguard alongside Mark's in preparation for a visit by Father Christmas. Soon three more were poking through.

'You see, Mammy,' said Martha, wishfully, 'Father Christmas might come while we are at church, that is, if you go to bed. He won't come if anyone's up.' It was always her hope that he would make their home one of his first calls, but it never happened. 'Perhaps he will, this time,' she thought.

Tom and his three children, well muffled in hats, scarves and gloves and wearing their best coats, made their way up the back field. They crossed the moor, went through the Mudhole, and walked down the tarmac road to Windrush. The air was sharp and cold with a light frost. The church was full. An air of excitement was almost tangible with whisperings and nudging among little children present. They were all longing to get home in case Father Christmas had been. Once Mass was over, the Holmes children couldn't get back quick enough, except for Emma. As much as she wanted to hurry, she found her feet dragging.

As they approached the Mudhole, she could no longer keep up with Martha and Tim. The gap between them gradually grew bigger. Tom waited for Emma, and slowed down his pace so as not to rush her, sensing that all was not well. It was a moonlit night and the snow glistened. Emma, crunching through the snow, thought that the crisp snowflakes were winking at her as the silver light caught their edges. A long line of footprints showed along the track where the older children had walked across the moor top and down the back field to home. Much to their disappointment, Father Christmas had not been. There were no bulging socks to greet them. There was only Mary, half-asleep in her rocking chair. She quickly made the children a hot drink and chased them to bed.

Martha and Tim woke up early.
'Come on, Emma. Come and see what we've got,' Tim shouted, excitedly. Emma did not feel like getting out of bed. Eventually, with curiosity overcoming her, she crawled out. Her arms and legs seemed wooden and heavy and she felt extremely tired. She pulled

on her cardigan and went downstairs but, showing little interest in her toys, she went back to bed. Mary was worried about her.
'She's sickening for something,' she said to Tom, when he came in after milking. 'She's not herself at all.' Emma was not hungry, either. No comment was passed when she asked for a very small portion of goose.
'I don't feel like eating,' was her explanation.

Emma went to bed early. Mary put her in a bed on her own as she was feverish. She tossed and turned most of the night and kept having dreadful nightmares.
'I can see it coming,' she mumbled, in her state of semi-consciousness. She could see a ghost sitting in the attic, with a long finger that wound its way down the wooden steps and under the door into Emma's bedroom. 'Mammy. Mammy,' she screamed, hiding her face under the blankets. Mary was soon upstairs to sooth her fretful child and mop her brow. 'Mammy,' screamed Emma, half an hour later. Mary padded upstairs again and found her daughter burning up with a high temperature.
'Mammy, I want a drink,' pleaded Emma. Mary went downstairs with her torch and went through to the back kitchen for water and took a cupful up to her daughter. The third time that Emma called out for a drink, Mary came upstairs and, after giving her a drink, put the cup down beside the bed.
'Do you think you can reach out and get it, Emma, if I leave you a torch?'
'Yes, Mammy.'

After a long, hot, restless night, Emma was pleased when morning came. Martha and Tim dressed and went downstairs. Emma could hear the clatter of pots and Amy crying, but she stayed in bed. Nobody came to call her. She was left to sleep. Eventually she struggled to put on her clothes and walked unsteadily downstairs. She pushed open the door and Mary gasped as she saw her.
'Oh, Emma, your face. It's all covered in spots. Go back to bed.'
Thankfully, Emma obeyed. The next time Emma opened her eyes, their family doctor was standing by her bed, smiling.
'It's the measles,' he said, and tuning to Mary, added, 'keep her warm, give her plenty to drink and no strong light on her eyes.'
The two adults went away but Mary returned shortly afterwards to draw the curtains and give Emma a few words of comfort.

Greener beyond the hill

It was a long Christmas holiday for Mary, but not of the usual kind. Emma spent many days in bed. Before she was well enough to come downstairs, Tim, Martha and Mark developed the measles and Mary seemed to endlessly walk up and down the stairs, with meals, drinks and bowls of water for washing, as well as having to sluice out chamber pots. When Emma was on the way to recovery and to save herself time and energy, Mary moved the other three children downstairs to the sitting room bedroom, to share the double bed. There they lay like three boiled lobsters, very red and hot and they became exceedingly irritable with one another, all being in the one bed. Mary found it difficult coping with the extra work and missed the help that the girls normally gave her.

Today Martha upset her bowl of soup and Mark accidentally let his jelly slip from his bowl onto the sheets. Amy was becoming very crotchety, whimpering or crying almost continuously. It was obvious that she was going to develop the spots. Mary buried her head in her hands and cried. She did not think she had the strength to continue. The constant demands of her children and the extra washing, as well as keeping the fires well stoked, were taking their toll. Tom missed his little helpers and spent more time doing all the small jobs that Tim and Martha normally did for him.

Mary sat in her rocking chair and sobbed. Amy crawled over to her and pulled herself to her feet to stand at Mary's knees. She was fretful and whinging. Mary reached out with one arm but could not contain her own crying. She'd had enough. Tom walked in, cold and tired, to find her very distraught.

'Come on, lass,' he said, tenderly, taking Mary in his arms. 'It'll be better soon.' He picked up Amy and held her close. 'Poor little bairn. You are hot. We'll put a single bed down here by the fire for her, Mary, so you can be with her more. She'll sleep a lot while she's ill and Emma will soon be up and about again and will watch her, for you.' Mary got up, wiped her tears and put the kettle on. She needed a cup of tea. She could hear Mark calling from the room.

'I'll see to him,' volunteered Tom. 'You just sit yourself down and enjoy that cup of tea. Pour me a mug out too. Then I'll sort that bed out for Amy.' He returned a little later. 'Po was full and Mark needed to use it.'

A day later, Emma was wandering around downstairs trying to help Mary. She was very pale and looked thinner. Mary thought she looked like a little orphan wearing the old, grey, cardigan that Mary gave her for comfort when she first took ill. Only three buttons remained from the original eight and the cardigan hung off her shoulders and almost reached her knees. Mary gave Emma a big hug. Baby Amy, now in bed in the kitchen, flung her blankets off and her fat, little tummy was so spotty that it looked like a Christmas pudding. Emma, sitting by the bed next to Amy and holding her sweaty, little fingers, began singing.
'Go to sleep, my baby. Close your pretty eyes.' The words drifted around the kitchen, a welcome noise to Mary's ears, as she realised that one child at least was over the worst and well on the way to recovery.

A quiet knock on her kitchen door startled Mary. She opened it, wondering who was walking in.
'Didn't see you at church and heard on the grapevine that your little ones were ill. Didn't like to knock loudly in case they are sleeping.' Jack Netherfield was standing holding out a packet.
'Just a few sweets for them. Can't stop. Hope they're soon better. Oh, and have you a cow syringe that I can borrow, please, Mary? I have a cow bad.' Mary took the sweets from him, went to the medicine cupboard and taking out a cow syringe, handed it to Jack. 'It's not actually ours,' she explained, 'but I don't think Charlie will mind you borrowing it. Bring it back when you've finished with it, please, will you?'
'Thanks Mary. I will,' Jack replied, graciously, and with that, he was gone, leaving Mary quite stunned. She thought he was so kind, but what should she tell Tom?
'Maybe not a good time to tell Tom,' she thought. 'It will bring back his anger. I'll wait a while. He's got enough worry at present.' Mary sighed. 'I'll have to tell him sometime though. Then what will happen?'

Greener beyond the hill

1948

'Now, Charlie, how's things?' Tom asked, hearing Charlie's voice as Charlie came striding up the cobbles. Charlie was calling to collect the milk as it was his turn and having spotted Tom heading for the coals door, called him. It was a bright, sunny morning. The two farmers stood for a few minutes in their black boots and navy overalls, in conversation. 'Come in for a cuppa,' invited Tom, as he opened the coals door.

'No, I haven't time. I'm a bit late as it is. Another time, maybe. By the way, have you got my cow syringe, Tom? I can't find it and wondered if you had it.'

'Aye, I think I have. Should be in medicine cupboard. I'll ask Mary to get it for you. I'll send one o' bairns across with it.'

They parted, Charlie heading for Tom's milk churns to load them on his cart and Tom going indoors and into the kitchen. The children were sitting at the table eating porridge. Four pairs of dark eyes met his gaze. Tom grinned at them.

'Grand to see them fit and well again,' he thought.

Mary was sitting feeding Amy who was perched in her high, wooden chair, strapped in with one of Tom's leather belts. She waved a spoon at Ted and tried to smile as Mary spooned in more porridge.

'I've just seen Charlie,' Tom said to Mary. 'He wants cow syringe. Can you send one o' bairns over with it?' Mary nodded. 'I'm off ploughing now. Tim, don't forget to clean pigs out. Martha, you can help him.' With these instructions, Tom left.

Mary looked in the medicine cupboard but couldn't see the syringe. She then remembered that Jack Netherfield called in after Christmas and borrowed it. With the worry of the children having measles, Mary forgot to mention this to Tom. She turned to the children.

'The syringe is at Jack Netherfield's. Which of you will go and fetch it for me?' she asked. There was no response to her question, the only noise being Amy banging her chair with her spoon. Tim didn't feel comfortable with Jack anymore, ever since that trip to Whitby.

'I can't go,' he said. 'I've got pigs to clean out. You heard daddy say so.'

'And I've got to help him,' added Martha.

'Well,' said Mary, turning to Emma, 'it looks like it will be you, Emma. Will you go for me, please?' Emma nodded. She didn't mind as she knew the way, having been once with Tim

'Better than cleaning pigs out,' she thought. Her only worry was that to get to Jack's farm meant crossing the field with the horses in.

'Be as quick as you can, please,' Mary said. 'I'll get one of the others to take it to Charlie's when they've finished doing the pigs.'

Emma ran off across the pasture and down to the beck. Soon she was crossing the bridge onto Jack's land. She stopped by the stream cupping a drink of water in her hands. It was cool and refreshing. She gazed down at the running water and saw hundreds of tiny tadpoles and lots of frog spawn. It didn't worry Emma that she was drinking this water. It tasted all right to her. The little tadpoles wriggled and slithered their black bodies around and around each other. Emma picked up a stick and prodded at them, making them move like lightening under and over the stones and pebbles.

Emma heaved a big sigh and after bending down to scoop another drink of water, set off again up the other side and over the stile. She walked along the side of a ploughed field before crossing yet another stile. Here, the view opened onto a large stretch of pasture. Emma was scared when walking through this field as there were three horses often seen galloping about and she was frightened they might trample her underfoot. She gazed around fearfully but there was no sign of the animals. She raced across the field and up over the gate at the far end.

'Now, just the dogs,' she thought. Tim explained when she went with him that sometimes they were fastened up, but other times they were outside and tied to a long, thick rope to allow for some freedom. Emma looked from left to right as she made her way to the farmhouse. There was no sign of the dogs. Emma was relieved.

She walked across the large, open, cobbled yard and timidly knocked on the door. She waited and knocked again, a little louder. She heard noises. The door opened slightly and Jack peered out. He didn't get many visitors and was suspicious when he did.

'Well, who have we here?' he said. Emma uttered her request.
'Come in and have a biscuit while you wait.' Emma followed him
in. 'I'll get you a drink. I won't be a minute,' he said, on leaving
the room.
'He doesn't look the same as he usually does, all smart and dressed
up,' Emma thought. 'He smells funny, too.' She felt anxious. She
sat down and looked around. There wasn't much furniture.
Everywhere was tidy and no toys littered the floors. Emma's mind
flashed back to her own house, a jumble of toys and paper, with
clothes pushed under cushions, and dust, inches thick, on the
mantelpiece. 'Still, it's home and we're happy,' she concluded.

She sat, swinging her feet back and forth, staring at the holes in her
shoes. She tucked them under the chair quickly when Jack came
in.
'There you are, lass,' he said, handing Emma the long, stick-like
object wrapped in brown paper. He gave her a biscuit and a cup of
milk. 'Tell your dad, thanks, from me.' Emma lowered her eyes.
'He doesn't know I've got it, does he?' he questioned.
'I don't think so,' Emma said, innocently, shaking her head.
'Well, we'll have to make the most of this,' Jack stated. Emma
drank her milk and ate the biscuit. She shyly thanked Jack and
made her way to the door. 'Wait,' called Jack. 'I'll give you a lift
in my van. It will be quicker than walking and your mam wants
that syringe as soon as possible, doesn't she?' Emma nodded and
waited by the door. Jack seemed to take a while getting ready.
When he re-appeared, Emma noticed that he was smartened up
with good clothes on, but she was worried about being late and
was relieved when, a little later, the van pulled up at Bankside
farm.

'Here at last,' said Mary, as Emma came through the open door
into the kitchen. It seemed quite a while since she watched, from
the kitchen window, her daughter run off in the direction of Jack's
farm. Jack followed Emma in. 'I thought I heard an engine,' said
Mary. 'It was good of you to bring her back. Will you stop for
some tea?' Jack nodded, taking a seat at the table.
'I think you deserve something for doing that, Emma,' said Jack,
smiling down at her and, putting his hand into his pocket, pulled
out a half crown that he handed to Emma. Her face lit up and her
eyes shone as she smiled up at Jack. Mary smiled. Jack stayed for

a while, chatting with Mary over a cup of tea and a cigarette. Mary enjoyed his company. She wished Tom would be more friendly with him.

Tom paused and was smoking a cigarette when he noticed Jack's van heading for their farmhouse but missed seeing Emma sitting in the front seat. He didn't want to break off from ploughing. He carried on, keeping one eye on the field and the other on the track. It seemed an age before the van pulled away. He resented Jack being involved with any of his family. He felt an undercurrent that he couldn't explain.

'Go and give this syringe to Martha and tell her to take it to Charlie's,' Mary told Emma, after Jack left. Mary was relieved to have it back.
'Little Drummer's banging at back door, Mammy. Have you fed him?' asked Emma. Mary sighed. She had forgotten with the fuss over the syringe. She went to get the bucket to fill it with milk. Little Drummer was a fine, young foal. He enjoyed his bucket of milk and banged his head on the pigs door if it was late. He was very tame and the children loved him. Emma found Martha and Tim and showed them her reward before giving Martha the message.
'Lucky thing,' her older sister said, enviously, wishing she'd gone.
'He's a nice man. I bet I don't get anything.' Tim pulled a face. He didn't agree that Jack was a nice man.

Tom was distracted for the rest of the morning.
'What was Jack Netherfield doing here?' he demanded to Mary over dinner. The children were all ears.
'I forgot to tell you,' stated Mary, 'that he'd borrowed the syringe. I sent Emma to fetch it and he brought her back.'
'He smelt awful, you know, Daddy,' said Emma, screwing her nose up for effect.
'I don't want any of you children alone with him again,' stated Tom. 'Do you understand?' he asked, his voice very stern. 'He must be drinking at all hours,' he continued, directing his comment to Mary. 'Don't send bairns over there again and you be wary when he comes creeping round here,' he added, as he got up and walked out. The children looked at Mary but she said no more. She was feeling sorry for Jack having no-one.

Weeks passed by for the Holmes family. They only saw Jack
Netherfield in passing at church. One Sunday afternoon, the
children were getting bored.
'Let's go to Charlie's to see May and Jake,' suggested Tim. It was
a beautiful day. The children were listlessly hanging around the
buildings whilst Tom and Mary were taking their afternoon nap as
was their habit on Sunday afternoons. Amy, too, was asleep.
'You can walk that far, can't you, Mark?' asked Martha. Mark
drew himself up to his full height and replied, very seriously,
'That's not far. I'm big now. I'm five. I can walk a long way.' His
large, brown eyes stared solemnly at his older sister. Martha
smiled.
'All right then, but you haven't to complain when you get tired.'

They set off at a good pace but Mark soon started lagging and
Martha, being motherly, hung back and took his hand. She knew
he didn't care much for walking.
'Come on, it isn't much further now,' she said, encouragingly.
'I want a drink,' sighed Mark 'I'm tired.'
'Aunty Dorothy will give us a drink when we get there,' his sister
replied, 'and maybe even a sweet,' she added, cajoling him. Mark
cheered up a little.
'Hey, wait for us,' Martha shouted to Tim and Emma, who were
away ahead. They waited and all four eventually reached the
cobbled yard, leading to the farmhouse.

'We've come to play,' said Tim, when the wooden door, with its
coat of grey paint, peeling off in strips, slowly opened to reveal
Jake, standing, open-mouthed and with his torn pocket hanging out
of his shabby, grey shorts.
'May, come and see here,' he called to his older sister and May
appeared in the stone-floored passage. Her black hair was tied
back and her pinny was hanging loosely over her short, cotton
frock. May's face puckered into a grin that seemed to emphasise
the dimple in her chin. Behind her, Aunty Dorothy appeared,
carrying baby George. He had traces of dinner around his lips. He
stared at the group with his dark blue eyes. Doris appeared next,
her long, mousy fringe hanging almost in her eyes. She was a
plump, sullen, little lass, almost three years old. With her stood
Dan, a tall, lanky lad with over-sized, hand-me-down shorts

hanging just above his knobbly knees. He grinned his lop-sided smile.

The Holmes children followed them into the sparsely furnished, large kitchen. Mark immediately sat down on the clipped mat and sighed.

'Can he have a drink, please?' asked Martha.

'Come on, our May, get them all a drink and fetch biscuit tin,' said Dorothy to her eldest child. It didn't take long for the children to finish their refreshments. 'Now, you can go out and play, you big ones,' Dorothy said. 'I'll put George down for his nap. Leave Mark here to play with Doris.'

When the older ones wandered outside, they discussed what to do. 'Let's go down t' wall over on far field,' suggested Jake. 'I can jump off it. I'll show you. I bet you lot can't,' directing this comment to his cousins.

'You shouldn't show off, our Jake. You're just a clever clog,' his sister, May, retorted.

'That's only 'cos you're too scared to jump,' he retaliated. 'Bet none of you dare.' The children argued and talked as they made their way across Charlie's fields to the farm boundary. They sat on the grassy bank near the wall that was partly broken down.

'Come on, show us, then,' urged Tim to Jake. Jake climbed up on to a solid part of the wall and took a leap into the air. He landed squarely on the grass below and stood up, smiling.

'See, I told you I could do it,' Jake said, triumphantly. Tim went next. He had no fear and landed safely back on the grass. The girls remained sitting, silently admiring the boys, as it looked a high jump. Dan was occupied trying to make a whistling noise by holding a grass blade between his thumbs and blowing. 'You're too scared, aren't you,' Jake said, teasing the girls. 'Girls are no good.'

'We're not scared,' retorted Emma, her independent spirit rising inside her.

'Go on, then, I dare you,' taunted Jake.

'Don't,' said May, looking very worried, as Emma stood up. 'You're too little.'

'You daren't, dare you?' gloated Jake.

Greener beyond the hill

Emma slowly walked up to the broken stones and climbed along the wall until she reached the highest part. She looked down at the grass below and fear crept over her.
'Go on. Go on,' shouted the boys.
'Shut your eyes and cover them. Then I'll jump,' shouted Emma. The children put their hands over their faces. In a split second, Emma leapt from the wall and fell awkwardly to the ground. She landed feet first. Her chin hit her bent knees with a crack. Emma let out a groan and rolled over.
'You shouldn't have dared her. You shouldn't have,' screeched May to her brother. 'It's all your fault.' Jake stared guiltily as he watched Emma get up, tears rolling down her cheeks.
'It's not my fault,' he said, feeling relieved that she had recovered a little. 'She didn't have to do it just because I dared her to.' Martha put an arm around her younger sister. She admired her bravery and was hoping she wasn't too badly hurt.

Tim spied Jack Netherfield walking over his land, divided from Charlie's by the wall that the children were jumping off. He nudged Martha.
'We don't want him coming over here. He'll want to take Emma home and dad will be furious,' he whispered to her. Martha nodded.
'Come on. We'll go home,' said Martha to her sister. 'You'll feel better soon.' They walked slowly back to the farmhouse and Emma's sobs subsided. She was feeling a little ashamed of crying in front of her cousins, but the pain around her jaw was becoming unbearable.
'Martha, you go and fetch Mark while I stay here with Emma,' Tim ordered his sister, 'and don't tell your mam and dad,' he added to May, Jake and Dan. 'Just say it's time for us to go home.'

Sometime later, as Mary and Tom were sitting drinking their tea, the four children wandered into the kitchen, the older three looking very sheepish. Mark was oblivious to what had happened. Emma hung back not wanting her parents to see her swollen neck but as Tom stood up to go out, he noticed his daughter's plight.
'Good grief,' he exclaimed. 'Mary, will you look at this.'
'What on earth have you been doing?' Mary asked, anxiously. For a moment, there was silence.
'Well, Mam,' started Tim.

'It was that wall, you know,' added Martha.

'We were jumping off it, and Emma fell awkwardly,' continued Tim.

'What wall?' questioned Tom.

'That one near the stack yard,' replied Tim. The children decided on their way home not to tell their parents the truth. They were told not to go wandering, unless Mary or Tom knew of their whereabouts, and they were warned about the broken wall being dangerous. Telling the truth would mean a telling off or even worse, a punishment. There was a wall, two feet high, near the stack yard surrounding a small paddock. This, they decided to say, was the one from which they'd jumped.

'Aye, I know it,' said Tom. 'You shouldn't have been playing such stupid games. She could have been killed. Get away out and get your jobs done.' Tim and Martha scooted out. Emma sat down on her Dad's vacated chair and remained silent.

'The least said, the better,' she thought. 'Thank goodness, Mark didn't see me jump. He'd blurt out the truth.' Outside Tim said to Martha,

"I hope Jack Netherfield doesn't go telling mam that he saw us. We'll really be in for it, if he does.'

During the next week, Emma remained at home. Her neck was so swollen that her chin was no longer defined and the bruising was very discoloured. Mary was not sure what to do about such cases. There was no hospital nearby. Tom, busy as always, said that it was probably just a case of severe bruising. One afternoon, the district nurse arrived. As Mark was now five and starting school in September, she called to check on his health. Mary showed her Emma's neck.

'What do you think?' she asked. 'Will it be all right? She only jumped off a low wall, but she cracked her chin on her knees when she landed.'

'She's a very fortunate little girl,' the nurse said. 'The way she landed, it's a wonder she didn't break her neck. She's had a lucky escape.' Mary took a deep breath and gave a sigh of relief.

'What worries, children bring,' she thought.

Later that day, Emma got her brother and sister on their own.

'Do you know what the nurse said? I could have broken my neck. Just think. It's a good job we didn't tell them where I really jumped.' Tim and Martha nodded.

'That's our secret, Emma, and don't you tell anyone, ever,' Tim stated.

'Perhaps when I'm a lot older, I might tell mammy,' Emma thought, 'but not for a long, long time.'

'Let's hope Jack Netherfield doesn't come calling. He's sure to say something,' said Tim, fearfully, still worried that his dad might find out that they'd lied.

One midmorning, a few weeks later, Mary was pouring a mug of tea for Tom's elevenses, expecting him any minute when she heard a vehicle.

'I hope it's not Jack Netherfield,' she thought. 'Tom won't be too happy.' She went to the coals door and opened it.

'Well, hello again. Much better weather now, isn't it?' was the greeting. Mary found herself gazing into the grey eyes of a smartly dressed gentleman, beaming at her.

It's... erm ...?'

'Dennis,' he offered.

'That's right. I was just bringing it to mind.' Mary noticed that his straggly beard was very neatly trimmed from the previous visit in all the snow and he now displayed a pencil thin moustache of similar colour. 'What a surprise. You've brought the sunshine with you, this time,' she added, smiling at him. 'Please come in. I'm expecting Tom any minute for his midmorning cup of tea. He usually comes in unless he's working over on the far fields. He'll be delighted to see you.' She turned and went back inside with Dennis on her heels.

A few moments later, Tom strode in, looking serious. As he saw Dennis standing by the kitchen table, his face broke into a smile. He visibly relaxed.

'I saw van and thought mebbee it was our neighbour visiting and that he'd changed his van. It's great to see you. Dennis, isn't it?' Dennis nodded.

'We said we wouldn't forget. Edmund couldn't make it as he's tied up with work but he helped to buy these. Just a little token of our appreciation for what you did for us,' Dennis added, handing a package to Mary. She placed it on the table and carefully opened it. Woodbines, a tin of salmon, gloves for the children plus a bag of sweets and a new pack of playing cards. 'I hope the colours suit and the sizes are okay.' Mary was lost for words. She picked up the tin of salmon and finally spoke.

'That is so kind of you. Such thoughtfulness. The gloves. The children are always in need of gloves. You couldn't have chosen better gifts than these. Our playing cards are getting decidedly sticky. We'll share the woodbines, won't we, Tom?' She added, laughing. Tom grinned.

'Very generous of you,' he said. 'We didn't expect anything. Did you get your car back?'

'Yes, we managed to rescue it a few days later. It needed a good clean but otherwise was fine.' Mary poured him a cup of tea and they continued chatting until Tom made a move.

'Back to work, I'm afraid. Thanks again, Dennis,' he added, holding out his hand. Dennis shook it firmly.

'I must be off too. Maybe, next time, I'll bring Edmund. Here's my address if you're ever in town,' he said, handing a piece of paper to Tom. Bye, Mary. Thank you for the tea.' The men walked out and Mary breathed a sigh of relief, glad that it wasn't Jack who'd visited. She was quite thrilled with the gifts.

It was during the summer holidays on a weekday that Martha was wandering anxiously around the kitchen.

'So, you think we can go, Mammy?' she asked for the umpteenth time. Mary glanced out of the window before answering her daughter.

'It doesn't look too promising, pet, but the weather forecast wasn't so bad. We'll see.' It was around this time of year when Mary put in great effort to take her children down to Beachcove to picnic on the sands and paddle in the sea. She did not care for the grit and dust on the sands but promised that, weather permitting, they would have their day out.

Martha's tummy felt peculiar as was usual when she was worried and excited at the same time. She wandered out to the toilet and sat on the wooden seat, thinking. She watched a spider spinning its fine web in the corner of the dust-ridden brick wall. Black beetles scuttled in and out of holes in the corners. A few woodlice lay motionless, like tiny pebbles, on the seat beside her. Martha longed to go to the seaside. She prayed for the weather to improve so that mammy would agree to take them. Coming back round past the open coal heap, she met Emma.

'Come on, mammy says yes. You have to help.' Emma had made a full recovery from her encounter with the broken wall and Jack Netherfield had not been to Bankside since. The children stopped talking about that day.

'Are we really going?' Martha asked, her face lighting up with pleasure.

'Yes,' replied her sister. 'So, come on.' Tim was dispatched to Crossbeck farm to inform Dorothy that they were going, as she usually came with her brood to join the Holmes family. Baby George might be a handful, but Dorothy knew the older children would enjoy it.

Emma and Martha rummaged in a draw of assorted clothes for a spare pair of knickers each, to substitute for bathing costumes. Mary shouted to them to find Tim's trunks, a pair he'd claimed from a box of second-hand clothes sent to Mary from her sister, Maureen. Tim was delighted to have proper swimming trunks.

'Put a pair in the bag for Mark,' shouted Mary. 'Find some knickers you've grown out of, Emma. They should do.' Emma and Martha giggled.

'Fancy wearing ours,' Martha said. 'They'll do, Emma, that navy pair. Elastic's gone a bit, but holes are all mended. Mark won't notice.' They were pushed into the bag.

'Shall we get towels as well, Mammy?' shouted Martha, very excited and longing to set off.

'Yes,' replied Mary, busily making sandwiches for their picnic. 'Don't forget some spares for Amy. She's not a bit reliable. You set off up the back field with Mark and I'll catch you up.'

Mary put cups and a bottle of diluted orange juice in the basket. She sorted out some stained, large spoons and dropped them in. 'Good for digging with,' she thought. Tim came dashing in.

'Aunty Dorothy's gone up road, Mam. I'll help you carry that. Dad's not coming, is he?' Mary shook her head. Neither Tom nor Charlie cared to join their wives for this excursion. Farmers did not go in for paddling in the sea.

'Among all those holiday makers, donkeys and wasps.' Tom said. 'Not me, lass. You take them.' Mary was not able to change his mind.

Half way over the moor, having struggled up the bank from the Mudhole and carrying Amy, Mary caught up with Dorothy.
'If it wasn't for bairns, I wouldn't bother,' Mary panted.
Perspiration was running down Dorothy's face as she nodded.
'They do look forward to it, though. Our Dan and May haven't stopped chattering about it since they got up early this morning as I'd told them yesterday that we'd probably be going. Never seen older ones do their jobs so quickly.'
'I thought the weather would let us down,' said Mary, 'but it's getting out nice now. Doesn't want to be too warm.' Mary smiled to herself. 'I sound like a farmer's wife,' she thought, 'talking about the weather.'

They made their way to the road, joining the children just before the bus was seen coming along. As it came to a halt, the six older children rushed up the steps and pushed their way to the back so that they could all sit together on the long seat. Dorothy and Mary clambered up escorting Doris and Mark whilst carrying George and Amy. Mary stopped to pay the driver.
'Look out for us this afternoon when you come back,' Mary said, smiling vivaciously at the young, fair-haired man, as she handed him the fare. 'I don't want to be left in Beachcove with this little lot.' The driver grinned and nodded.
'Rather you than me,' he said, winking at Dorothy. She beamed. Her mousy hair was hanging in damp ringlets over her perspiring brow. The bus pulled away. Mary gave one or two nods to passengers, acknowledging their greetings, as she struggled up the gangway with Amy and the basket, following Dorothy and the little ones.
'Room up here, Mrs Holmes,' called a man from the back. 'Going t' sands, are you? You'll be all right, weather wise. Forecast's not bad.' Mary nodded. She decided it was a necessary obsession with farmers. If they listened to nothing else, they always made a point of hearing the weather forecast on the wireless.
'Just like I do,' she thought, wryly.

The children were enjoying their journey.
'Look. There's our school,' shouted Tim, pointing, as the bus rumbled past St Peter's school opposite the church. 'I take my eleven plus exam next year,' he continued. 'My dad wants me to pass and then I'll go t' grammar school.'

'I'm going to be a farmer like my dad,' said Dan. 'I don't like school.' The bus made a few stops on the way, depositing passengers and letting some on. It was becoming crowded.

'Look, Martha, how steep it is,' said Emma, fretfully. As the bus crawled slowly along, she could see the road dropping sharply before them. She gripped the seat in front and hardly dared to breathe as the bus approached a very tight corner whilst grinding its way to the bottom of the hill. It pulled to a halt at the bus stop in Beachcove.

'We're here,' said Dorothy, with a sigh of relief. Mary and Dorothy struggled up to the front of the bus with their belongings and the little ones, at the same time calling the older ones to follow.

'I can see it. I can see it,' shouted Emma, her voice rising in excitement. The sea seemed enormous, mile upon mile of water, with waves breaking as they reached the shore. Numbers of sunbathers were scattered along the sand in little groups. The two families climbed down from the bus and tasted the salty air as they gazed out to the sea.

'Now hold hands and don't set off until I say so,' said Mary.

Just when they were about to move, a car came tearing around the corner at great speed and screeched to a halt. Mary turned and saw Jack Netherfield's van. He'd spotted them and, wanting to stop and talk to Mary, braked sharply. Unfortunately, Jack was driving too fast and when he pulled up, the van mounted the kerb. He lost control and the van swerved, slightly catching a young girl who stumbled and fell to the ground. Jack was horrified. He climbed out of the van to be greeted by a middle-aged lady.

'You stupid man. You stupid man. You could have killed her,' the woman shouted hysterically, her arm around the little girl, now back on her feet but crying, her ice-cream lying splattered on the pavement. Jack began to apologise but the woman turned her back and walked away holding the little girl's hand. Dorothy kept the children back, as Mary, having given Amy to Martha to hold, went over to the scene.

'I only want to talk to you,' said Jack, shakily, breathing alcoholic fumes at her. Mary took a step away from him, feeling physically sick. 'Can I come down to the beach with you for a while?' She nodded, a little reluctantly. She felt uncomfortable around Jack when he'd been drinking. 'I'll just go and park the van.' He got back in and drove off whilst Mary re-joined Dorothy and the children.

'By, that could have been nasty,' said Dorothy. 'Now, we'll go together,' she instructed the children. Mary felt quite shaken up inside, not mentioning to Dorothy that Jack would be joining them, as she didn't want word getting back to Tom, through Charlie, that she was encouraging him.

The party moved onto the beach where the soft sand gave way under their feet. Once on the sands, the older children scampered ahead delighted to have arrived, the light breeze carrying particles of sand across their faces. Dorothy mentioned to Mary that the tide was going out.

'We'll have a good few hours and we won't be cut off,' she stated. A suitably sheltered part under the rocky cliff side seemed an ideal place for some privacy and the party settled down to take off shoes and socks.

'Can we go and paddle, Mammy?' asked Martha.

'Yes, but don't venture too far,' Mary instructed. Martha and Emma ran to the sea edge and watched the water roll in and cover their toes. It was cold. May paddled further in and held up her skirt to keep it dry.

'I'm going back to change,' shouted Martha. 'Come on.' They raced back up the beach and quickly undressed.

'Shall we take Amy?' Emma asked.

'No,' replied Mary, busy tucking her tiny daughter's skirt inside her knickers. 'She will stay and dig with Doris, but you might take Mark for a paddle.' George was asleep and Dorothy put him in the shade of a jutting out piece of rock face. The older children flung their clothes on top of their socks and shoes and tore off back to the water, Martha dragging Mark along with her.

Mary spotted Jack stumbling across the sands. He came over to them, nodded at Dorothy and sat down beside Mary, the stench of alcohol permeating the air around him. Jack started rambling on to Mary as he pulled out his cigarettes and lit one from a lighter.

'Your Tom's a lucky man,' he said, dragging deeply on his cigarette. 'I've got nothing. No wife, no bairns, nothing, but he's got everything. But then he always did have.' Mary looked at him. He'd obviously had another drink after he'd parked the van. He was slurring his words.

'What do you mean, he always did have?' Jack was picking up sand and letting it trickle through his fingers, acting as if he'd never heard her question.

'It's not right someone having everything and the other person having nothing,' he mumbled. Mary didn't understand what he meant but she could see he was in no fit state to make any sense. 'One of these days, he'll find out what it's like,' he continued, with another drag on his cigarette.

'Find out what's like?' Mary asked, beginning to lose her patience. 'Jack, you're not making any sense.'

'No, maybe not,' he said, struggling to his feet. 'Well, I'll be off now. See you sometime.' With that, he wandered off in the opposite direction to the way he came.

'Poor man,' said Dorothy, sympathetically. 'He's so upset about that little girl.' Mary said nothing. She was convinced Jack's troubles went much deeper that.

Emma was listening to the waves hitting the rocks further down the beach. She watched a motorboat tearing through the water, giving off a spray whilst its passengers waved to the bathers.

'Shall we have a donkey ride, Tim?' asked Martha.

'You can, but I'm going to build a castle.'

'I'll help,' shouted Emma. 'Let's make a long channel down to the sea.' There was so much to do. The sun came out and the warmth of its rays gave added pleasure to the children as they dug and scooped and patted the sand into place. Calls from the grown-ups were ignored until they realised that they were very hungry.

'Let's go and eat. Race you,' Martha said to Emma. They ran back and fell in a heap on towels and clothes.

'Careful now,' said Mary, 'or you'll have sand in everything.' It did not seem to matter to the children that their bread was rather gritty. Jake and Dan found some seaweed.

'What are you going to do with it?' asked Tim.

'My dad says if you hang it up, you can tell when it's going to rain,' Jake answered. Dorothy explained.

'When its wet, it going to rain and if it's dry, you have good weather.'

'Farmers and weather again,' Mary thought, ironically.

'I'll go and get ice cream cornets for us all. You lasses, come and carry them,' said Dorothy, pulling herself to her feet. Emma,

Martha and May returned each with a handful of cornets, the ice cream melting and dripping down the sides. Mark dropped his and his mouth started to quiver.

'You can't eat it now, son, it's all sandy. Here, have mammy's,' consoled Mary, passing him her ice cream. She did not want anything to spoil their day out. She thought, at one point, that Jack might, but to her relief he hadn't come back. After the children finished their ice creams, Dorothy took them to the toilets. It was a fair walk, but the children were delighted when, on the way back, she bought flags to stick in their sand castles along with a couple of buckets and spades. Emma decided that Dorothy must have quite a bit of money as she paid for the ice creams too.

Emma was more surprised when they returned to their spot on the beach and saw Mary pulling out her purse.

'Who wants a donkey ride?' Mary asked. Tim and Martha decided to go along with May, Jake and Dan. 'Don't you want one, Emma?' Mary asked. Emma shook her head.

'I'll go with them and watch.' It did not seem very safe to her, wobbling about on the backs of animals. She watched a boy crying before he was lifted off. She felt sorry for the donkeys going backwards and forwards all day long and thought that some of the children looked too big and heavy for them.

'Was it good then?' Mary enquired of Tim, who was the first to climb down.

'It was,' he said, 'and now I want to make a better castle.'

Soon it was time to pack up.

'Can we have just one more paddle, Mammy?' Martha asked.

'Go on, then, and wash the sand from your arms and legs. Fill the buckets with water so that I can rinse the little ones' legs.' The children raced down the beach. It was much further to go as the sea was moving away, or so it seemed to Emma. Mary watched them, their little heads bobbing up and down among the sun-seekers and family gatherings. Mary smiled. 'It's been so worthwhile and they'll sleep well tonight,' she thought.

Getting dressed was quite a performance. Tim wandered off to find himself a secluded place behind a large rock. He did not care to be watched. Mary and Dorothy held up towels around their children in turn, to save them from embarrassment. It was not very successful, but the girls and boys felt that they were being protected from onlookers and each another. They quickly rubbed themselves dry and then changed out of wet, bedraggled knickers into dry ones.

'Come on, Mark,' called Mary. She caught him and pulled off his unusual 'trunks', rinsed his legs with the sea water from the bucket and gave him a brisk rub down before dressing him.

'We'll walk up to the bus stop and put our shoes and socks on when we get there,' said Dorothy, 'otherwise we'll go home with half the beach in our shoes.' A tired party, armed with seaweed, pebbles in buckets and broken flags, clambered on the bus. Amy was fretful. She'd only taken a short nap on the beach and was tired. Mary sank into a seat and gave a deep sigh. She was glad it was all over.

That evening, Tom listened to the chorus of voices telling him of the lovely time they had spent on the beach.

'You would have liked it, Daddy,' Martha said.

'Think so, lass?' he asked, smiling at his rosy-cheeked daughter.

'It was great, Dad. I went on a donkey and we had ice creams, big round ones,' informed Tim.

'Mark dropped his,' added Emma, 'but mammy gave him hers.'

Tom smiled over their heads at his wife.

'It was a success, then?' Mary nodded. She was mulling over the day's events.

'The children seemed to have forgotten the incident with Jack,' she mused. She hoped it stayed that way.

'Come on, let's have you all to bed,' said Tom, getting to his feet. When Emma climbed between the sheets, she was very, very tired. She lay back and closed her eyes. She could see the waves rolling onto the rocks. She could hear the sea and the motorboats. She sensed the joy of running in bare feet over the sand and letting the cold water cover her toes, her feet slowly sinking. She fell asleep with a smile playing on her lips, full of contentment after a lovely day.

1949

With it being not such a hard winter, Tom stared his spring work a little earlier than usual, but his sheep were lambing, increasing his workload. More and more, he relied on his children to help him. 'It never takes them this long to come home,' Tom said, angrily, to Mary, as he appeared at the kitchen door yet again. 'It's quarter to five and they're still not here.' He was waiting for his children to come in from school to give him a hand as he was behind with his work. He'd spent hours searching the moortop for a ewe that was missing. When he finally discovered her on her back in a ditch, it was too late to deliver her lamb safely. His lambs were very important to him as they made money at the sales later in the year. Every lamb saved was money for foodstuffs for winter.

Today, Tom found two stillborn lambs. The cold, March winds were a hindrance to his work, as the sheep seemed to disappear in search of shelter. Tom was vigilant with his animals but it was an impossible task to be always checking on them. At lambing time, sheep were often checked four times a day.
'I don't understand how that sheep got down there. They never wander down that part,' he said to Mary, chewing over the loss of the lamb, he'd delivered.
'Which part's that?' she questioned.
'You know. Down by rocks near beck adjoining Netherfield's land.' As Tom spoke, it began to dawn on him that maybe the ewe wasn't there, by chance. 'He wouldn't be driven to stoop so low. He's no reason to,' thought Tom. He voiced his doubts to Mary. 'You don't think Jack Netherfield will have anything to do with it, do you, Mary?' Mary knew Jack was bitter towards Tom. She recalled his words, *Why should he have everything and me nothing? One of these days he'll find out what it is like.*
'Well, I suppose if he got drunk, he might,' she ventured.
'I'll walk over one night and see him,' stated Tom. 'Meanwhile, as soon as they're in, tell bairns to get out and get jobs done. I'm going back t' sheep again. I have another lambing.'

Mary sighed.
'Poor bairns. He is a bit hard at times,' she thought. She supposed he was worried. She heard the pigs door open and the chatter and noise as her children came in. 'Where on earth have you been? Your dad's real mad with you. You'd better get a move on. Get

changed and get your jobs done, after a quick bite to eat. It's five
o'clock. It never takes from half past three to this hour to come
home.'
'We stayed and talked at road end and played hide and seek,'
Martha explained.

Almost an hour later, Tom strode in. He looked stressed and tired,
his brow furrowed and his lips tight.
'Pot of tea, love?' asked Mary.
'No thanks, I haven't time. Lost a sheep this time. I found it in
beck near where I found other one. Seems odd to me. They never
go down there. If its anything to do with that Jack Netherfield, I'll
kill him. Anyway, I've put skin off dead lamb on motherless lamb.
I hope dead lamb's mother will take to it. Bairns getting jobs
done?' Mary nodded. This was another farming practice she learnt.
A sheep won't take another's lamb. To convince a mother sheep
whose lamb has died that another lamb is her own, the dead lamb
is skinned and the coat is fastened over a lamb without a mother.
Sheep have a strong sense of smell and because of the skin from
their dead lamb, covering the motherless one, they accept the
lamb. After a few days, the skin is discarded.

Before going to bed that night, Tom warned his children.
'If you're not in by half-past four, tomorrow, I'll wallop you all.
Mark can walk it in an hour. Now, I've told you.' The next day,
Thursday, was the fortnightly delivery day when a travelling van
brought loaves of bread to the Holmes family. The loaves were left
in a basket at the top of the bank leading down to Moorbeck. This
saved the delivery driver having to open and close the last two
gates. The children picked up the bread on their way home from
school if Tom hadn't time to collect it.

Tim, Martha and Emma dawdled and chatted along the road side
on the way home from school. May, Jake and Dan sauntered up
the grass beside them, with Mark lagging behind. He was tired.
When they arrived at the road end, they sat down for a rest. Emma
loved swinging around the signpost. It gave her a sense of
freedom, gliding through the air, just her fingertips on the post to
keep her balance. They set off at a slow pace over the moor. Down
through the Mudhole they tramped. Tim climbed over the
boundary gate.

'You're not supposed to do that,' said Martha. 'You know daddy says it's bad for the gate.'

'I've just remembered,' Emma gasped. 'We're in trouble if we're not home by half past four.'

'Oh, heck,' said Martha. With great speed, they rushed up the other side, dragging Mark along, and started running over the rough grassland.

'I know,' said Tim, 'you and I will carry bread, Martha. Maybe dad will think that's why we're late.'

'I want a loaf as well,' demanded Emma. They arrived at the gate at the top of the bank and sorted out the bread. Tim and Martha carried the large basket between them. Emma ran off down the hill with a loaf under her arm. 'Mark won't get hit,' she thought. 'He's too little.'

She walked into the house, nervously, wondering how late it was, and if Tom would be waiting. He was and he was angry.

'Put it down,' he ordered and he walloped her once on her bottom. Emma screamed, more with shock than pain, and ran back outside to hide in the lavatory. When Tim and Martha arrived, they received the same treatment. Tim gritted his teeth but Martha cried a little.

'I don't know how you can do it,' said Mary, later in the evening. 'I have to, lass. It was after half four and I'd warned them. They must learn that I mean what I say. You don't think I enjoy it, do you? They won't do it again.' Mary remained quiet. Unlike Tom, she wasn't used to a tough farming upbringing. She felt their children struggled enough with the harsh conditions without that sort of punishment but she supposed that he was right. She thought about it and suffered mentally for quite some time.

It was after nine o'clock the same evening when Tom set off to Jack Netherfield's. He'd been chewing over what he might say to Jack, whilst doing the milking. He hadn't enjoyed walloping his bairns. He was angry with everyone including himself. When he reached Jack's farmhouse, he hammered on the door.

'Not again,' he thought, as he heard noises from within. Eventually the door opened and as Tom expected, Jack had obviously been drinking.

'What do you want?' were his opening words.

'It's about one of my sheep,' Tom started.

Greener beyond the hill

'Aye, I heard about your sheep,' slurred Jack. 'Well, don't come bothering me with your problems. You don't know the meaning of hardship. Be off with you. Go on. Go and tell someone who cares.' He swayed in the doorway. He lurched over and slumped to the floor. Tom was sickened. He knew a conversation at this point was impossible. Jack reached out for Tom to help him up but Tom turned his back and walked away, leaving Jack cursing and swearing.

'I hope he chokes on his own vomit,' Tom thought, angrily, as he walked home.

May half term arrived and with the children on holiday from school, Tom voiced a suggestion.

'How about we go and see dad tomorrow, Mary?' He was standing with her in the orchard, watching the children rolling around in the grass. 'It's his birthday soon and he hasn't seen his grandbairns for ages. We'll tell him about new one on way.'

'That will be great, Tom,' she replied. 'I like your dad.' The baby was expected later in the year and Mary was hoping that threshing day would be over before it arrived.

Friday dawned, sunny and warm. Tom arranged for the milk lorry driver to pick them up at the road end. He was a local guy and willing to help and was happily whistling away whilst sorting out the milk churns when the Holmes family turned up foot, their own milk churns having been delivered earlier by Charlie.

'You go in cab with Mark and Amy,' Tom instructed his wife. He lifted his older children over the sides to stand at the back with the churns and hauled himself over to join them. 'Now hang on,' said Tom, as the engine started. 'No leaning over sides.' The children hung on tightly to the rope that secured the churns. They had a bird's eye view of the countryside, the farmhouses, the hedgerows and the animals that dotted the fields. They were delighted with this way of travelling. Tom was feeling content, too, looking forward to seeing his dad and returning to the farm where he was born, now run by his elder sister, Gertie.

'Been a long time since you were over,' Gertie greeted him, coming across the cobbles. She pointed out the cows grazing in the nearby field, very proud to show her younger brother her farming

achievements. She recounted her many hours spent single-handedly milking, cleaning out and working the land.
'You should see my muscles. Like a fellow's, they are,' she boasted, proudly. Mary nodded and smiled. 'Dad doesn't do much now,' she continued. 'He's getting too arthritic. I'm gaffer now.'
Mary felt sorry for Tom's dad, all alone except for Gertie. He was a tall, grey-haired man, with bushy eyebrows overhanging his deep blue eyes. Mary found him to be such a kind, gentle-faced person, softly spoken and gracious. He was sitting in his usual place by the fire in his armchair in the corner of the large, stone-floored kitchen, his two sheep dogs lying down, one at either side of him.

Mary walked up to the old man and gave him a kiss. The children did likewise. He was immensely pleased. His blue eyes twinkled. Mary whispered in his ear and he smiled again, looking up at Tom.
'Are you going to have a lad, then, to even it up?'
'We'll have to wait and see,' Mary replied.
'Off you go and play outside while I get dinner on,' Gertie said, waving the children out. They all went like sheep, meekly following one another, Martha holding Amy's hand. Nobody argued with Gertie.

It was over dinner that Tim remembered his news.
'Have you told granddad about me, Mammy?'
'I'll tell him, lad,' Tom replied. 'We're very proud of our Tim. He passed first half of his eleven plus exam. He'll be off to Whitby grammar school in September, if he passes second half. Teacher thinks he will.' Granddad was delighted. His children were not well schooled.
'They're clever, are they, as well as good looking? Must get it off their mother,' he teased. Mary smiled again.
'You are lovely,' she said. 'I'm sure some of it comes from Tom.'
Dad liked this young woman that his son married. She was refined, intelligent, and very charming. His mind wandered back many years.
'She's like my Josie,' he thought, 'but that's my secret.' He smiled to himself.
'Come on, Dad, wake up,' said Gertie.
'I'm not sleeping,' he answered, indignantly. 'I'm thinking.' The afternoon passed quickly. The children played in the yard and in the woods, whilst Tom pottered outside with his dad. He knew his

dad was very lonely and had been, since Tom's mam died many years ago.

'I'll try and come again, soon, Dad,' Tom said, as they parted. 'Aye, do that, lad. It's been a grand day. Take care of that lovely lass of yours. She's given you a fine family.' Tom's dad stood on the step and waved, until the family were out of sight. They made their way along the cart track to the road where another local farmer on his way to visit a relative in Windrush, was picking them up in his van to take them home. As Tom ushered his children into the back of the van, Mary put her arm around his shoulders.
'He's a grand old man, your dad, Tom. We don't go enough.'
Tom agreed and made a resolution that he would make a real effort to visit his dad more often.

The long summer days stretched into autumn. Mary was glad the children were back at school. Tom took Amy with him in the afternoons whenever possible to enable Mary to have a rest. Amy was not as tall for her age as her two older sisters. Her hazel-coloured eyes shone brightly under her pencil thin eyebrows and she was very cute with her cheeky smile.
'Mammy's getting fat, Daddy,' she said, one afternoon, as they left Mary settled in her rocking chair.
'Aye, she is,' Tom replied. 'You're going to get a baby brother or sister soon.'
'You mean like when sow had its babies, Dad? Will mammy have lots, then, Daddy, like sow?' Amy asked, wonderingly. Amy remembered being lifted to peer over the pigsty door to see the old mother pig and her ten babies.
'No, lass, only one, I expect,' replied Tom, grinning at her. 'We'll get threshing day over with, first, I hope.'

The threshing machine was pulled from farm to farm by the heavy tractor. Tom arranged for it to be brought to Bankside farm, early one Saturday afternoon. His uncle Sam was coming to help, along with the local farmers, as many hands were needed to help on a threshing day. It was the day Mary hated, as she was expected to feed about fourteen men. Instead of sleeping lately, she was churning over ideas for baking. She dreaded it all, remembering the hours and hours she spent in previous years, rolling pastry, filling pies, and making sponges and buns. This time it was going to be worse as she was already weary, being heavily pregnant.

'I think, Tom,' Mary said, a few hours later, when he walked in with Amy, 'I'll keep Martha and Emma off school on Friday to help me bake and to mind Amy. I just don't think I'll get through on my own.'

'That's a good idea, lass,' replied Tom. It won't matter keeping them off school for once.' Emma and Martha were delighted to hear that they could stay at home to help. They enjoyed baking. Emma often armed herself with pinny and the Bero recipe book and, amongst other choices of cake recipes, made ginger loaves. She made mistakes, like the time she accidently used pepper instead of ginger when making a pudding. Placing on the table a steaming hot, ginger pudding, Emma waited in anticipation for the compliments. The family still talked of Tom's outburst when he took a large mouthful.

It was a busy baking day. Martha, needing lots of patience, allowed Amy to make a hole in each jam bun and plop in a spoonful of jam. Flour soon spread to hands and faces and the floor. Mary wondered whether it was worthwhile having them off school.

'You aren't supposed to eat it, Amy,' she shouted, in exasperation, as Amy stuffed uncooked pastry into her mouth. 'Take her away and clean her up, Martha. Emma, you clean up that mess.'

Mary's patience was at an end. She wiped a floured hand across her brow. A tear trickled down her face. Her legs and feet ached. Her back was painful and she felt enormous. Amy anxiously walked up to her mammy.

'Don't cry, Mammy,' she whispered. 'Emma and Martha will wash up.' More tears of self-pity welled up in Mary's eyes. She dragged Amy up onto the little knee space that was available and cradled Amy's head on her swollen tummy.

Emma went and brought the washing-up bowl from the back kitchen. Martha poured out boiling water from the kettle. 'I'll wash and you dry,' she said to Emma. Her sister nodded. They were both subdued. They did not like to see their mammy cry.

'It's that big baby, isn't it? Does it kick you a lot?' Martha asked. Mary smiled through her tears. It was difficult to explain to her children all the emotions felt during the last weeks of pregnancy. 'No, love, I'm just tired. You've been good girls,' she said, reassuringly.

Next morning, Emma and Martha were up bright and early. Immediately after dinner, they scrambled into their boots and coats before rushing out to see the threshing machine. There were men all over the stack yard. Tom and Charlie came out of the farmhouse carrying mugs and a milk bucket full of tea, for the farmers. The girls watched in amazement. Some men were sitting on the grass enjoying a smoke whilst others were standing around talking or inspecting the lots for sale. Tom, using his own pint mug, began ladling pint after pint of tea from the bucket, for the men. Tim appeared with a basket filled with buttered scones. When the men finished drinking, they returned the mugs and cups, some cracked and some without handles, for Tom to carry back to the house in the empty bucket.

'You'll want this one, I reckon,' said a voice Tom recognised. He turned and saw Jack Netherfield standing before him.
'I don't want you on my land,' said Tom, his threatening tone attracting attention of those nearby.
'Now, Tom, I've just come to help, being neighbourly,' said Jack, placing his mug in the bucket. They stood face to face, the other farmers watching and waiting with interest. Tom did not want to cause an ugly scene, with everyone around.
'Jack,' said Tom, calmly, 'just go quietly. I don't want your help. You've done enough damage.' Jack stood there.
'I'm just honouring the local custom, Tom, and anyway, what do you mean, I've done enough damage? Have you any complaints against me?' he asked, innocently, his eyes laughing at Tom, taunting him. 'You're jealous of me because I take your Missus out in a van and you can't afford one,' he continued. 'You can't give her what she wants and she turns to me.' Jack was flowering the situation, relishing in the increased speculation of the onlookers.

Tom was outraged. He glared at Jack's deep blue eyes.

'Who do they remind me of?' Tom questioned himself, but his mind was too blurred with anger to recall where he'd seen those eyes before, on someone apart from Jack. Tom saw Mary out of the corner of his eye coming towards him. She was coming for the used pots, wondering why the delay in bringing them to her. Tom wanted to keep things under control as he did not want Mary upset in her condition. 'All right. Stay this time,' he said, begrudgingly. 'I might as well have some work out of him, for nothing,' he thought. Tom turned his back on Jack and carried the pots into the house. Mary followed.

When the farmers settled to work, Emma, too shy to do so earlier, made her way across the grass to stand and watch. The large tractor, like a great monster, was sending forth, deep, thundery noises as its engine worked the conveyor belts on the threshing machine. The noise was intense. She cupped her hands over her ears as she drew nearer to the huge pieces of machinery. Men were cutting the sheaves of corn and feeding them into a drum. Here the corn was knocked off and went down the riddles as it was cleaned of chaff. Emma slowly walked the length of the threshing machine and watched the corn coming down spouts into rows of bags, hooked on and slowly filling. As soon as a bag was full, one of the men removed it and carried it to the barn whilst another bag was hung in its place.
'Don't go too close, Emma,' warned Charlie. 'It's dangerous if you get too near.'

Emma suddenly spotted uncle Sam riding down the track on his pushbike and ran off to meet him. The children liked him very much, not least because he always brought a huge bag of mixed sweets to be shared out amongst them. Uncle Sam was popular with Mary also. He was courteous to her and patient with the children. Uncle Sam parked his bike alongside the house, whilst listening to Emma chattering away beside him. They walked into the kitchen to be greeted warmly by Mary, who, after uncle Sam took off his coat and sat down, made him a hot drink.
'Tom will be pleased to see you,' she said.

They chatted together a little, but it wasn't long before she needed to start packing up the tea for the threshing men. Uncle Sam went out to join the men, returning later to eat with Tom and Charlie and one or two others. For the rest of the workers, Mary placed pie upon pie and buns and cakes by the dozen and many sandwiches, into the basket.

'All that hard work,' Mary thought, 'and it disappears in a trice.' Another full bucket of tea was brewed and taken out again with the cups and mugs. It was an extremely busy day, not only one that farmers were pleased to see the back of, but their wives, even more so, were relieved when threshing day was over for another year.

The following day, Emma was having her last nurse on uncle Sam's knee before he left.

'Can I come with you please?'

'I can't take you. I've no room on my bike.' Emma thought for a moment.

'Well,' she said, 'I could always run behind.' She considered herself to be a good runner and convinced in her own mind that this was quite possible to do. Her parents joined in the laughter with uncle Sam.

'You're a tough little nut,' her uncle replied, 'but I think it's a bit far even for you.' Tom thought it was a gem. Another one to tell his mates over a pint in the pub.

It was later in the day that Mary brought up Jack Netherfield's name in conversation with Tom, when Tom was having a mug of tea. She was pondering over the scene in the stack yard, the day before, when she went out to collect the cups, seeing Tom and Jack standing face to face, as if they were challenging each other. She was curious as to their conversation but waited until uncle Sam left before mentioning it to Tom.

'You had a great turn out of farmers yesterday, Tom, with their offers of help. A good day for you. I was wondering about you and Jack, though. You seemed to be in earnest conversation with him but neither of you looked like it was a friendly talk. Something serious, was it?' Tom was silent for a moment.

'How much should I tell Mary?' he thought. He knew she wouldn't be happy knowing that he'd ordered Jack off their land especially after Jack volunteering to help with the threshing. He knew Mary felt sorry for Jack. She was vulnerable herself at present, being heavily pregnant and quite emotional at times.

Mary waited, realising that Tom was finding this difficult.

'It's okay if you don't want to tell me. I was just curious, really.'
'Forget about it, Mary,' Tom finally replied. 'We had a few words but that's all. I don't think there's much love lost between us but the day ran smoothly and that's what counts, and he stayed to do his bit. It's over now.' With this, Tom drained his mug of tea and went back to work. Mary wasn't so sure if that was the end of it, though.

Greener beyond the hill

1950

'Does it really make washing easier?' Tom asked the assistant. He was on one of his trips to Whitby and was looking at some washing machines. Tom had been debating for some time about washing machines, knowing that Mary spent hour after hour, scrubbing and rubbing, especially since the arrival of their sixth child. He was proud of his baby boy, Jacob, another dark-haired, brown-eyed infant. Over the winter months, Tom was determined to ease Mary's workload as soon as money permitted.

'Yes. You fill it with hot water. You put the washing in and add the powder and push the handle back and forth. This rotates the washing and it cleans beautifully,' the assistant gushingly explained. Tom pondered. Martha and Emma could push that lever to and fro. He would buy it. He pulled out his cheque book and signed.

'You can deliver it,' he informed the assistant. 'Road in has been improved a lot.' The rough track passed Marsh farm into Moorbeck was much firmer since the repairs, making it less of a problem for drivers to drive their vehicles into the valley. The washing machine arrived the following Saturday and was tried out immediately.

'Will clothes come out all ready to hang up, Mammy?' asked Martha.

'No, love, we'll still have to rinse them but we won't be scrubbing them like we have been doing,' Mary explained.

The children were fascinated by this new piece of equipment, but even more so when Tom told them he was going to buy a tractor. Tom spent some time mulling over aspects of their life style. He knew that he could not do much about the tilly lamps, but as well as buying a washing machine for Mary, he was seriously considering buying a tractor.

'It means borrowing money but at least a tractor won't lie down and die like a horse does,' Tom reasoned to himself. This is what happened to Blossom, their third horse to die in less than eight years. 'Mary is delighted with her washing machine,' he thought, 'and I'll have a tractor,' he decided. Tom was behind with the farm work. He felt he'd made progress over recent years by building up his stock and farm tools even though he still borrowed hay rakes and other implements. A tractor it would be.

'We must be getting rich,' Emma whispered to Martha. 'We're actually going to have a tractor.'

'What's it like, Dad?' Tim wanted to know.

'Well,' said Tom, pensively, thinking how best to describe the tractor he was purchasing. 'It's red and has a double seat.'

'Yippee,' chorused the children. 'We'll be able to ride on it.'

'We will, won't we, Dad?' asked Tim, hesitantly. Tom nodded and smiled.

'When I've learnt to drive it,' he replied, grinning at his excited children.

The day arrived when Tom collected his tractor. He picked it up from a garage at Shepton, Charlie having dropped him off in his van, and drove the tractor over minor roads and moorland until he reached the far side of Moorbeck above Crossbeck farm. Down the steep incline, he rumbled. Looking over the valley, he could see his family outside the coals door waiting patiently for his arrival. Tom smiled and glowed inwardly. His boots were well worn and his tattered jacket was fastened with a piece of binder twine, but despite these outward signs of poverty, Tom felt like a king. He pulled up near the cobbles at Bankside farmhouse and turned off the engine.

Mary, carrying baby Jacob in her arms and surrounded by their other children, walked over to him.

'Oh, Tom,' was all she could say. 'This was such a proud moment in Tom's life,' she thought. Many farmers used tractors and some even owned cars. To buy his own tractor meant much to Tom. Mary was so pleased for him. The children's faces were pictures of delight.

'Dad, it's smashing,' said Tim. He was growing tall and learning well at Whitby grammar school, having passed his eleven plus exam as predicted by his teacher.

'You'll have to learn to drive it, lad,' Tom said, as he climbed down from the double seat. 'No more walking to church, Mary, or pushing pram. We'll go on tractor.'

'Will we, as well, Daddy?' piped up Martha.

'Aye, I should think so,' he reassured Martha, 'but I'll have to think how you'll all fit on.' With that, the family trooped into the house for tea, full of high spirits and excitement.

'With washing machines and tractors, life is looking up,' Mary thought, quite contentedly.

Tom was true to his word. At first, he only took Mary to church on the tractor, parking it on the village green alongside the vans and cars of the more affluent farmers. Eventually, he allowed one or two of the older children to stand on the bar at the back and hold on tightly to the seat. The splashes of wet mud and water that sometimes flew up behind the children's legs or clothing, especially when going through the Mudhole, were left to dry and were brushed off later. The bright, red tractor became a common sight, chugging its way down the tarmac road. Word got around the village that Tom Holmes had bought himself an 'Express' after Nick Edwards benevolently and with a wry smile, named the tractor thus, in front of a small gathering outside church one Sunday morning. From then on, adults and children alike, referred to Tom's tractor as the Moorbeck Express. Over the weeks, Tom found time to make a detachable, small, wooden, platform with sides, that he fastened to the link bar when taking his family to church. This was safer for the younger children to travel in provided they held on tightly to the sides.

The Sunday arrived when the Holmes family all went together to church on the tractor for the first time. Tom and Mary sat on double seat with baby Jacob being nursed. Tim and Martha stood, one each side of the large mudguards. Emma, Mark and Amy climbed onto the wooden platform at the back. They were off. At fifteen miles per hour, they chugged their way over the moor and down the road waving to any pedestrians they overtook and to passing cars. The Moorbeck Express was parked with great pride on the village green and the Holmes family climbed down to join other parishioners going into church. After Mass, Tom drove his family to the village Post Office and General Dealers. He waited whilst Mary and the children, apart from Tim, went inside to buy The Farmers Weekly and purchase a few sweets.
'He's a little smasher, isn't he?' said Mr Stoutly, smiling at Mary with Jacob in her arms. Mary nodded, before ushering her children out to where Tom and Tim were waiting, and they all climbed back onto the tractor.
'Are you going for a drink, Dad?' asked Tim, hopefully, knowing that if his dad went, the children would get a drink of lemonade.
'Please, Daddy. Please,' shouted Martha. Tom eyed Mary and she nodded.

'We might as well make the most of our outing,' she thought. The children were pleased. Tom nodded, revved up his tractor and made the short journey to Hunters Lodge. After parking his tractor on a stretch of open grass outside the public house, alongside the parked cars, Tom and Mary, with baby Jacob, went inside. It wasn't long before Tom brought out lemonade for the children. 'We won't be long,' he said, before going back in.

'He always says that,' complained Martha, after Tom disappeared, 'but he takes ages.'

Eventually, Mary came out first, carrying Jacob.

'Just a few more minutes,' Tom shouted after her, as she left the pub. Mary was ready for home.

'Your dad will be out shortly,' she said to the children, a little listlessly. 'He's just finishing his pint.' She heard the pub door open and glanced to see if it was Tom.

'Hello again, Mary,' Jack Netherfield greeted her as he sauntered over.

'Waiting for him, are you?'

'Yes, he won't be long.'

'Fine looking vehicle, he's got there. Not as comfortable as a van but better than walking, I guess.' Jack pulled out his cigarettes and offered Mary one.

A little later, Tom, having enjoyed immensely his two pints of beer and a game of dominoes, came out to find Mary and Jack engaged in an intimate conversation. Tom felt the bristles on the back of his neck stand on end.

'Come on, lass,' he shouted to Mary, ignoring Jack, as he climbed onto the tractor. Mary and the children clambered to their places without a word.

'What's the matter, Tom? Why are you so rude, ignoring Jack like that?'

'What's the matter?' Tom said, repeating her question, angrily.

'What do you think is the matter? You stand there chatting him up. Can't you stay away from bloke?' he retorted, furiously.

'Oh, Tom, you know I wasn't. I'm not like that,' said Mary, defensively, her face reddening.

'Well I don't care. I don't like you talking to him. You don't know him like I do.' With that comment, he pursed his lips and said no more.

'Oh dear,' thought Mary. 'What a way to end our trip out, but I do think Tom is being unreasonable.' Mary was justifying her friendly chat with Jack to herself as she rather liked him.

The Express was a great asset. Tom used it for pulling the plough and the chain harrows, taking the milk and meeting Tim from the bus when he was laden with shopping. Mary sometimes wondered how they ever managed without it. She learnt many new words like gears, choke, and TVO (tractor vaporising oil). There were times when the tractor nearly let them down. Martha, who hated being late for any event, detested Sunday mornings when Tom went to start the tractor and the engine wouldn't turn over. When that happened, he freewheeled the tractor down the steep pasture, helped on its way by willing children. On these occasions, Martha prayed for it to start and she knew her plea was being answered when she heard the roar as the tractor sprang into life, with Tom, turning it round and charging back up the hill to pick up a thankful family who knew it was too late for walking.

One Sunday after Mass, Mary, holding Jacob, was chatting with Mrs Featherstone.
'I'm sorry that Martha failed the second half of the eleven plus exam, Mrs Holmes,' the teacher said, 'as she's a bright girl. I was so delighted when Tim passed last year, the first child at St Peter's to do so for some time. I had high hopes for Martha, but never mind. We'll wait, hopefully, for Emma to succeed next year.' Mary nodded. 'Jake is a bright boy, too. Perhaps I'll have two successful pupils, or maybe even more,' Mrs. Featherstone added, optimistically, with something of a smile relieving the stern appearance of her wrinkled face. Mary smiled too. Perhaps the predictions might just come true.

As Tim was now old enough to be trusted to go to Whitby each Saturday to shop, he was unavailable for work on the farm that day, leaving Martha and Emma to work in the fields. It was the time of year when weeding turnips was one of their chores. Up and down between the rows, very slowly on hands and knees, the girls crawled, pulling out the weeds that surrounded the growing turnips. The hot sun blazed down on them as they spent hours tearing at the spreading, green plants that almost choked and buried the young turnip shoots. Behind them, the girls left a flattened mass of dying weeds, withering under the heat of the sun.

The girls found it easier on their knees if they scattered the pulled weeds on the soil in front and crept over them, but even so, their skin became scrubbed and cut, through contact with pebbles and rough soil. Their hands were covered in soil and their nails became chipped and dirty. The turnip rows stretched endlessly in front of them. When they reached the top of the field, the girls turned around and worked downhill.

'You know, Emma, I sometimes think my nose is going to hit the ground,' Martha said, as she crept very slowly down the steeper parts. The work continued in the early evening after school but Tim was excused because of his homework.

'I hope I pass my eleven plus next year,' Emma thought. 'I'd rather do writing than this.'

A more pleasant job was working in the hayfields. After Tom cut the hay and it dried out in the sun, he turned it into long, heaped rows. The girls helped to fork it into haycocks. Walking through a field of haycocks, Tom could easily pick out the ones his daughters put up. They were small and very uneven. Some had lost their tops altogether because the hay was cocked too loosely and it needed only a light wind to lift it off. Consequently, there was a scattering of loose hay around numbers of haycocks. Martha and Emma worked hard at this job but developed many blisters on their fingers and palms, the result of their hands sliding up and down the fork handles.

At the end of a late evening, they helped to get the cows in for Tom and each milked one or two. Martha was very good at milking, but Emma's fear of animals hindered her efforts. Her three-legged stool with its very wobbly leg added to her problems. Even the cows seemed to sense her stiff, tense body as she sat under the animals with blistered fingers, trying to get squirts of milk into a bucket.

'I don't think I'll ever be a farmer's wife,' she thought. Her little body ached. Her eyelids were heavy. Her open blisters were sore. She prayed that the cow would not kick.

'Off you go in, lass,' said Tom, as he walked up to her. 'I'll finish that one. Tell your mam to clean up those hands with disinfectant and you get off to bed.' He bent down and took her bucket, as

Emma slowly stood up. She picked up her stool with one hand and flung her other arm around Tom's neck and kissed him.

'Good night, Daddy. God Bless. I'm so tired tonight.' Tom smiled. 'She's a real little trouper,' he thought. 'They all are.'

After the summer holidays, Martha, Emma and Mark were delighted to discover that they no longer had to carry their bait bags to school. Progress was being made at St Peter's school in that a cooked dinner was provided every day. Mary was overjoyed. The children came home with descriptions of jam roly-polys and rice with sultanas.

'It's all served out properly, Mammy,' the girls explained, 'in big tureens.' This was a new word to them. The Holmes children were served at home straight from pans.

'We can have second helpings, as well,' added Mark, who loved his food.

'It doesn't seem to spoil your appetites at night,' Mary replied. The children, after their walk home, were ready for any warmed-up leftovers from the dinner time meal of Tom, Mary and the little ones. With not having bait boxes to put up for the children, Mary found that the jam pasties, rock buns and fruit pies lasted longer. She was pleased that she did not need to bake quite so often.

Autumn became winter. Early each morning, Martha and Emma struggled to dress by the flicker of candlelight whilst Mary lit the coal fire downstairs. The school children huddled around it, getting what warmth they could from its little yellow flames that struggled for life through the black coals. It was dark outside as they made their way up the back field early, to go to school, the cold, raw air rushing into their lungs. Mark was sometimes given a helping hand by Martha or Emma as he climbed down and up the slopes of Mudhole. Tim left earlier to catch the school bus to Whitby. The children were always glad to be home in the warmth of the farmhouse kitchen.

One Friday evening, a few weeks later, Mary was sitting at the table with her cracked hand mirror propped up against a mug, trying to apply her lipstick. Mary and Tom were going dancing, a very rare occurrence. Mary was wearing her smart, black dress, with a red rose brooch pinned on the front. She felt classy with silk stockings and black, shiny shoes. Her dark, curly hair was shining.

She looked at her daughters, kneeling on the mat in front of the crackling fire, watching her, their faces enthralled. Martha thought her mammy was beautiful and Emma thought her mammy looked like a lady.

'That's what I'm going to be when I grow up,' she confided in Martha. 'I'm going to be a lady.' Tom came downstairs dressed in his grey, pinstripe suit. He had dusted down his light, black, dancing shoes, and combed his thick, dark hair, now sleeked back and shiny. He stood to attention.

'Will I do?' he enquired. Mary smiled, thinking how attractive her husband was.

'Oh, Tom, you look grand,' she enthused.

Tim walked in through the door.

'I've finished outside.' He stared at his dad in amazement. 'Dad, you do look good.'

'Don't I too?' asked Mary, petulantly.

'Yes, Mammy, you are real pretty,' Tim answered, smiling at her. On the rare occasions that Tom and Mary went out together, elaborate plans were made for baby-sitters. Tonight, for the first time, the three oldest children were going to be left to guard the home and look after the younger children.

'Don't forget,' said Tom, 'that you mustn't move the fireguard or touch the fire.'

'And,' added Mary, 'lock the middle door when we leave.' There were no locks on the outside doors of the back kitchen, only snecks, but the middle door to the passage and kitchen had a heavy, strong lock, rarely used by the family. Tim nodded.

'We'll be all right, you know, Dad. I'm not frightened,' he said, reassuringly.

Tom was looking forward to a drink and a dance, as he was feeling sad over the loss of Little Drummer. The colt was always such a fit, active animal, never ailing a thing. Having been weaned off his bucket of milk, he was free to roam the pastures. It was a week ago, that Tom was first concerned because he hadn't seen Little Drummer. He went for a walk over the fields to see if he could spot him, and eventually, found the colt dead, sprawled under a hedgerow, with eyes glazed open. Tom was mystified. He called out the vet who said that Little Drummer must have eaten something disagreeable. Further investigations would reveal more of the stomach content but Tom couldn't afford them. He dug a hole near to where the other horses were buried and asked Charlie to come and help bury Little Drummer.

'Now, that's strange,' said Charlie, when he was shovelling the earth into the grave. 'Are you sure it was early Thursday you found him?'

'Aye,' said Tom. 'Why?'

'I was up early that morning. We'd had a restless night with George. I looked out and there was a fellow walking over your pasture. I thought it was you, same tall build and striding walk, but on second glance, I saw it was Jack Netherfield. I thought at time it was odd that he was on your land at that time of day. I meant to mention it sooner.'

Tom mulled over this conversation for days and decided to have a closer look at the pasture to try and find out what Little Drummer could have eaten. He searched up and down the hedgerow. A few yards from where he discovered Little Drummer's body, Tom found a few crusts of half eaten bread. He picked them up, inspected them more closely and sniffed them. They were laced in rat poison. Tom was furious.

'Who the hell poisoned one of my horses?' he asked himself. His mind flashed back to Charlie's words, *I saw it was Jack Netherfield.* Tom was livid, convinced that Jack must have done it deliberately. Tom wouldn't put it past him. 'Why would he do this? What have I ever done to him? I'll kill him,' Tom fumed, instinctively. 'But I've got no proof and colt's buried,' his thoughts continued. He considered further. 'Maybe one o' bairns fed Little Drummer with crusts with poison, that I'd put down to kill rats. They wouldn't know crusts would harm him.' Tom felt foolish for thinking it was Jack. He hated Jack but felt that this was a little extreme even for him. Tom dismissed the death as an accident, not mentioning it to any of the children. Little Drummer was dead. The children would be upset if they thought they'd killed him. Tom was annoyed with himself. What a waste of a good working horse. He would need to be more careful in the future. 'I'm not having much luck with my horses,' he thought.

His mind came back to the present. He was eager to get going. 'About ready?' he asked Mary. They were off to the dance. She nodded and bent down to let her little girls kiss her.

'Just on my cheek,' she said, 'or you'll spoil my lipstick.'

Edna Hunneysett

'You smell lovely, Mammy,' said Emma.

'We'll be good,' added Martha. Mary and Tom walked out, followed by Tim, who turned the lock in the middle door after them. The children settled down for a long evening.

'What shall we do first?' asked Martha. She found it strange without their parents and rather exciting.

'Cards,' replied Tim. They played game after game until boredom set in. They decided to have a drink of milk and a sandwich. The draughts board came out and, as usual, Tim, taking the girls on, in turn, was the winner each time. The fire died down but the children had strict instructions not to poke it or put on more coal. The light from the tilly lamp was dimmer as it needed pumping up to revitalise it but the children remained seated, Martha in the rocking chair and Tim on Tom's armchair. Emma curled herself up on the clip mat.

'You know,' said Tim, 'if we stay very still and quiet, a mouse will come out of that little hole in the skirting board. I've seen it happen before.'

'Really?' said Emma, becoming more alert, as her eyes were starting to close.

'Just watch,' said Tim. They remained silent, hardly daring to breathe. The only noise came from the quiet hissing of the tilly lamp. Martha's eyes were glued to the hole in the skirting board and suddenly she saw a little, whiskery face with two beady eyes. The mouse came out and ran along the fireplace. Immediately, Ginger, the cat, shot across the mat, but could not get to its prey because of the fireguard. The mouse scuttled back into hiding, behind the skirting board at the other side.

'Poor old Ginger, you missed your supper,' said Martha, disconsolately. Emma sighed. Having recovered from that little excitement, her eyelids began drooping again.

'Move on a bit,' demanded Tim. 'I want to put mam's slippers to warm. She'll like that.' Shuffling along a little, Emma closed her eyes. It wasn't long before she was asleep. Tim placed the slippers near the fireguard and, after checking the door to make sure it was locked, settled back in his chair. He closed his eyes, as did Martha. Everything was quiet except for the ticking of the clock on the mantelpiece.

Two miles away, in the village hall, Tom and Mary were finishing the evening with last waltz, gliding effortlessly around the remaining couples on the dance floor, Dorothy and Charlie amongst them.

'It's been such an enjoyable evening mixing with the locals, socialising and dancing with different partners,' Mary thought. She particularly enjoyed her buffet supper, being waited on by some of the ladies from the village. People were drifting away after collecting coats from the cloakroom.

'Good night. Goodnight,' was heard as folks wandered off to their homes. Tom and Mary followed Charlie and Dorothy to Charlie's van. Charlie opened the double doors at the back and Tom and Mary climbed in.

'My feet,' complained Mary, pulling off her high heels and putting on her flat shoes. 'That's better. What a grand evening. Such a nice break. You almost forget what it's like to let yourself go and enjoy yourself, don't you?' Tom nodded, enthusiastically. The van pulled up at bottom of the bank at the approach to Bankside farmhouse and Charlie let Mary and Tom out of the back.

'Goodnight,' Mary called, as she linked arms with Tom. Thanks for the lift.' They sauntered along the track and over the cobbles.

A few minutes later, they reached the coals door, tired and ready for bed. They went in and Mary tried the middle door. As she expected, it was locked. She knocked hard. Tom joined her. He hammered on the door.

'Let's walk around to the window,' suggested Mary. They went outside and around to the front of the house to peer in through the dirty panes. The fire was out and the lamp was very low, but Tom and Mary, adjusting to the light, could see three sleeping children. Tom knocked on the pane. Mary shouted, but not too loudly as she did not want to waken the little ones. Eventually, Tim stirred and opened his eyes. He smiled vaguely at his parents' earnest faces pressed on the window pane. 'Tim. Tim,' Mary said, urgently, knocking on the window again. 'Open the door and let us in.' Tim opened his eyes a second time. He gazed at his parents, unable to clear his fuddled, tired brain. Tom called him.

'Come on, lad. Open door. Let us in.'

Something was stirring in Tim's mind. He looked at where he was sitting and then across at his sleeping sisters.

'I must have gone to sleep,' he thought. Tom was watching him intently. He could see that Tim was coming to.

'That's right, lad. Now open middle door,' he said, encouragingly, more to himself than Tim. Tim stood up as if in a dream and half fell across Emma. She stirred and settled down again. He staggered to the kitchen door, fumbling with the sneck. He reached the middle door and turned the key back. Mary and Tom walked in. 'Off you go to bed, lad. Thanks a lot. Can you manage?' Tim nodded. He walked drunkenly to the stairs door dragging his tired body up to bed.

'Fancy,' said Mary. 'They've even put my slippers to warm. How thoughtful.' Tom picked up Emma and carried her to bed. Mary undressed her and covered her up as Tom brought his other daughter to her.

'They won't remember a thing in morning,' said Tom. 'They've done well. Growing up you know, aren't they, when we can leave them sitting for us.' Mary nodded. She was very tired. Acknowledging that her older ones were no longer little ones, was a happy and sad feeling. She checked on the three youngest before getting into bed. As she drifted off to sleep, clasping Tom's hand, she was back on the dance floor, exhilarated and excited, reliving the pleasure of a rare night out. Tom was also feeling content because, before they went to the dance, he was concerned about how to react if Jack Netherfield was there asking Mary for a dance. Luckily, Jack never turned up.

It was back to the humdrum of work the next day with the memories of the previous evening evaporating quickly. The children were argumentative because of their late night and constantly bickering. Mary was wondering whether the night out was worth it.

'Maybe I'll try and visit Tom's dad sometime soon,' she thought. 'Charlie would take me. Something to look forward to.'

Greener beyond the hill

1951

Life was easier for Tom and Mary with the washing machine and with the tractor. Tom's herd of cattle increased in numbers producing a greater milk yield resulting in bigger milk cheques at the end of each month. Mary found an outlet for her creative talents by joining the WI (Women's Institute) enabling her also to have some social life. Dorothy went with her and although it meant a few miles walking there and back, they were happy to have some time away from home each month. Dorothy enjoyed singing, with Mary accompanying her on a little, old guitar, given to her many years ago, by her father. They entertained members of the WI with their musical duets. Once a month, Mary faithfully attempted the competition, be it creating a Christmas novelty, a flower arrangement, special cakes recipe, and even a decorated coat hanger. Another outlet for Tom or Mary were the whist drives held in local villages. Infrequently, they managed to attend one and enjoyed a social get-together as well as improving their skills at cards.

During this year, Mary and Tom received notification of Emma passing the first half of the eleven plus exam. She was to attend a venue in Whitby to sit the second half along with Jake and three other girls, one of whom attended the Church of England school in the next village but lived in Windrush. Mrs Featherstone was delighted with the success of her pupils and personally arranged for the five children to be taken by car to Whitby, a rare treat for Emma.
'What was it like? Was it hard? How did you get on? Did you finish the papers?' The questions were endless when Emma returned home.
'There was a piece about a man eating corned beef, Mammy, and the question asked what corned beef was. I finished all the sums. They were quite easy but there was a word that I didn't know.'
'What was it?'
'Well, it was horizon,' said Emma, putting the emphasis on the first *o*.
'Oh, Emma, you pronounce it horizon, and you don't know what it means?' Emma shook her head.
'No, but I managed otherwise.' Mary explained the meaning of horizon to her. 'I wonder where I'll go if I pass,' Emma mused.

Tom and Mary also wondered. Tom was worried about the expense and how they could possibly afford to send Emma to a grammar school if she passed.

The day finally arrived when the buff envelope was delivered to Bankside. Emma thought she was going to be sick with anticipation.

'You've passed. You've passed,' shouted a delighted Mary. There was jubilation in the farmhouse kitchen before Mary and Tom settled down to read the remainder of the letter. It was much later in the day when Mary asked Emma a very important question.

'How would you like to go to a boarding school, Emma?' Her daughter, pushing back the clip that was sliding out of her straight, silky, black hair, slowly churned the idea over in her mind. She remembered one or two very old books of Mary's about boarding schools. There were stories of pillow fights and midnight feasts. She thought of the different things she would have chance to do like going to swimming baths and playing tennis and making new friends. Boarding school life, as described in the books she'd read, sounded very exciting.

'A boarding school,' she thought. This was beyond her wildest dreams but Emma knew that her parents had little money. 'I think I would, Mammy, but how? You can't afford for me to go to a boarding school.'

'You passed your eleven plus exam, Emma. That means, because we don't have much money, the council will help with a grant to pay for you,' Mary explained. 'They've given us a list of five schools. We think Scarborough convent grammar school will be best because you can board there. Daddy and I will write about you going.'

A few weeks later, Emma and Mary were sitting in the back of Father Burnett's little black car with Tom in the front. The priest, dressed in black and wearing his biretta, was chatting to Tom whilst puffing his pipe as he drove through the villages on the way to Scarborough. Father Burnett watched the Holmes children growing up. When he heard that Emma was to have an interview at the convent to see if she was suitable and acceptable as a pupil at the school, he offered to take her with her parents in his car. His Irish brogue was delightful. His light blue eyes twinkled as he spoke. Father Burnett visited the family at Bankside from time to time and suspected that Mary and Tom would find going to

Scarborough and the convent, an ordeal. Hence his generous offer.
Emma was nervous as she thought of her interview and even more
so, when the car pulled up in Queen Street.
'Here we are. I'll see you later. Good luck, Emma. Mind you
speak up,' said Father Burnett, as he opened the doors for his
passengers to alight. Emma gazed in awe at the tall, sombre, large
buildings surrounded by very high, spiked railings. The priest
waved goodbye to Mary and Tom and drove off to meet his
colleagues at St Peter's after making the arrangements with Tom
to meet up with the family for dinner.

The small party walked up to the very large, wooden doors, on
which, for a handle, was an enormous ring. At the side of this ring
was a small shutter to allow the occupant to see out before opening
the door. Mary pulled on the ring, triggering a loud, clanging
ringing inside the convent. The shutters moved before the door
opened wide and Mary and Tom stepped inside, followed by a
trembling Emma. She gazed around her, quite speechless. She was
standing in an enormous hall with a spacious corridor leading off
on either side. There were large, wooden, double doors opposite,
that she learned later, led to the chapel. The floor gleamed. There
was a polished, double seated bench on either side of the front
door.

A chubby, happy-looking nun, wearing glasses, was smiling down
on her. Other nuns were gliding past dressed in long, black clothes.
They tucked their hands under a narrow, blue piece of material
resembling a lengthy scarf reaching from their neck band to their
black, lace-up shoes. Black headgear rested on their shoulders with
a white band covering their foreheads allowing only their facial
features to be seen. Emma couldn't take her eyes off them. She'd
never seen clothes like this in her life. Tom and Mary introduced
themselves and were ushered into a side room to wait.

Later in the day, Father Burnett was told all about the interview,
having driven the family to a hotel to treat them to a meal. Emma
was amazed at the quantity of knives, forks and spoons in front of
her.
'There are loads,' she thought. 'What will I do with them all?
Which ones do I use?'

'You start at the outside and work in over,' the kindly priest said, noticing her dilemma. 'Just copy us. Don't worry about it.' Tom and Mary told Father Burnett that they thought the interview went successfully, especially with Mary explaining to the interviewers how difficult it would be for Emma doing homework in their overcrowded kitchen. This was an ongoing problem for Tim after starting grammar school. Mary told the panel she felt it would be to Emma's advantage to be able to work and read under the supervised conditions that the convent was offering.

'One of the nuns very gently took hold of Emma's shoulders and pulled them back,' laughed Mary. 'Our Emma always hunches up when she's nervous. The nun said they'd have those straightened out. They'll make a lady of her yet,' added Mary, looking down at her daughter's flushed face.

The journey home passed like a dream for Emma. She later related her day's experiences to Martha. Martha was a little worried about the future in store for her younger sister. They had never been separated before.

'It will be different without her,' thought Martha, sadly. Within a few days, the letter arrived confirming that Emma was allocated a boarding place at the convent grammar school. Jake passed the eleven plus exam too, and was going to attend a grammar school in Middlesbrough. Charlie was delighted about Jake.

The weeks flew by. Although the fees for the convent school were covered by a grant, Mary was obliged to provide bedding, uniform, and clothes for Emma to change into, in the evenings and weekends. The expense seemed endless.

'You can't afford it, Tom,' said Nick Edwards, one Sunday morning outside church when Tom was telling him about the expenses for Emma.

'Well, I know where to come if I get stuck,' stated Tom, to his very good friend. My bairns will do all right.' Nick nodded. He had supported Tom financially, on a temporary basis, a few times in the past. Tom repeated this conversation to Mary, later in the week, when she was distressing over the money situation. They bought a large, expanding suitcase for Emma. Mary painstakingly listed the most necessary items of clothing needed from the original list of the suggested and required garments and bedding. 'It's not as if I can put her old clothes in. She hasn't much decent to wear,' Mary said to Tom. Soon Emma would be leaving for

Scarborough and not be returning home for seven weeks. Amy joined Mark at St Peter's in Windrush leaving only little Jacob at home with Mary, toddling around and getting under her feet.

'I think I'll ask Charlie to drive me over to see your dad,' she said one morning to Tom, a few days after Emma left. 'We missed his birthday and I want to tell him about Emma, how Tim is doing, and what a little trouper Martha is helping you on the farm. I'll show him how Jacob has grown, you know, all the family stuff. I'll go today while you are at Whitby. I'll be back before the children are home from school. What do you think?'
'Okay, lass, whatever you like. I'll be off.' He kissed her and Jacob and hurried out to walk to the road end to catch the bus to Whitby. Not long after Tom left, Jack Netherfield, out in his van, was driving along the same road and spotted Tom waiting at the bus stop. He decided to take the opportunity to visit Mary. He sometimes spoke to her at church, but hardly ever got chance to spend time with her.

'Hello, Jack,' said Mary, as she opened the coals door on hearing a knock. 'I was just about to leave.' Jack's heart sank. 'I'm off to ask Charlie to drive me over to see Tom's dad.' Jack was silent for a moment and appeared to be deep in thought.
'I'll tell you what, Mary,' he began. 'It's a shame to bother Charlie when I'm here. How about me taking you? We'll be back long before Tom gets home.' Jack knew Tom wouldn't approve of him taking Mary, but Jack didn't care. He wanted to be with Mary and for some time he'd been wanting to visit Tom's dad. He was delighted to have this opportunity. Mary pondered for a moment. 'It won't matter if I go with Jack,' she thought, 'and it will save time.' Jack was waiting for her reply. 'All right,' she replied. 'Great,' responded Jack. He picked up the toddler and carried him to the van. Mary followed.

It wasn't long before they arrived at the farm. There was no sign of Gertie. Mary walked in, the door being unlocked, followed by Jack who was carrying Jacob. Dad was sitting in his chair by the fire with his two dogs. He looked up as Mary approached and reached out his arms. Mary kissed him.
'Who's brought you here, then? Nothing wrong is there?'

'No, Dad, of course not,' she replied, to his relief. 'I just wanted to see you and give you all the news. Tom's always so busy. I've brought Jacob,' she said, taking the toddler from Jack. 'You've not seen him since he was a baby.'
'Aye, that's right. You had another lad to even things up, didn't you,' Dad said, jokingly. 'He looks like Tom, a chip off the old block, he is. And who's this fellow?' he queried, standing up and offering his hand.
'This is Jack Netherfield, a neighbour. He kindly offered to bring me here,' Mary replied. The two men shook hands.
'I think, Mr Holmes, that you knew my mother, Josie Archer,' said Jack. The older man's face froze as the colour slowly drained away. He gazed, with his blue eyes into Jack's blue eyes, looking for answers. He sat down again.
'Are you all right?' Mary asked, placing her little boy on the floor and kneeling to take Dad's hand. 'Can I get you a drink of water or something?'
'Just one of my funny turns, love,' he answered, the colour slowly returning to his face.

He looked up at Jack and lowered his eyes. He picked up Jacob and placed him on his knee. Jack remained silent. Mary chatted on about Tim and Emma and how helpful Martha was for Tom. She told him about Amy joining Mark at St Peter's school in Windrush.
'I only have this little one at home,' she said. Jack didn't join in the conversation. He stood and stared at the tired, old man.
'I think you better be off now,' Dad said to Mary. 'I need a rest. It's been grand seeing you. Come again and get Tom to come too.'
Mary kissed him. She picked up her toddler and made her way out. Jack and Dad looked at each other once more, but neither spoke. Jack turned and left.
'He didn't seem himself today,' said Mary, getting into the van. 'I hope he's not getting sick.' Jack was very quiet as he drove.

'Jack, you're going the wrong way,' said Mary, suddenly.
'Come back to my place for a cup of tea, Mary?' Jack requested. 'I have something to tell you.' Mary was concerned at this offer. She always found him very pleasant but Tom was suspicious of him and she was uncertain about what she should do.

'Just for a short while,' she replied, thinking, 'I don't have a choice. He's driving there anyway.' She reasoned that she could always walk home from his farm if she wanted to leave.

Jack pulled up at his farm gates. Mary got out of the van, opened them and, after the van went through, closed them. Taking her little boy from Jack, she walked up to the front door. In the sparsely furnished kitchen, Mary sat down. Jack brought Jacob a biscuit. He produced a bottle of whisky and two glasses.
'Have a drink with me, Mary?' he asked. Mary shook her head. She wasn't expecting this. He sat down next to her. He filled one of the glasses and downed the whisky in one gulp. He reached out and took her hand. Mary withdrew it.
'I think I'd better be going, Jack,' she began, but Jack interrupted. 'No, listen, Mary. I'll make you a cup of tea. I must tell you something that's been bothering me for a while.' He lit a cigarette and poured himself a second glass of whisky. He drank it swiftly before getting up to put the kettle on the fire.

'When I met you, Mary,' Jack began, 'you reminded me of my mam. Attractive and chatty, warm and sensitive. I envied Tom. Why should he have everything and me nothing, I thought.'
'What do you mean, Jack? Tom has everything. I don't understand.' Jack didn't answer. He handed the little lad another biscuit. The kettle was boiling and he made a cup of tea for Mary. She was feeling uneasy. She cuddled her son closer to herself.
'I'll have to go, Jack,' she said. 'I can walk home.'
'No, let me finish,' Jack said, his voice becoming slurred. 'I love you, Mary.' He leaned forward until his face was almost touching hers. 'You are so pretty and clever. Stay with me. He's not good enough for you. I'll look after you and your bairns. Leave him. Come and live with me. I'll make you happy,' he continued, placing his hand on her cheek. Mary flinched and pulled away, too frightened to speak. 'I wanted him to look badly in your eyes. I wanted him to fail. I want you, Mary. It was me who poisoned Tom's colt and killed that sheep of his, anything to see him downgraded.' Jack stopped talking, still looking at Mary, waiting for a response. Mary was aghast.
'I must go,' she said, determinedly, rising from her seat, but Jack stood up and reaching out his hands, cupped her face with them.

He was so close to her that Mary could almost taste the cigarette smoke and whisky on his breath.

Meanwhile, Tom arrived home from Whitby. He was surprised to find no-one at home. He made himself a cup of tea and put the shopping away.
'She must be over at Charlie's,' he thought. 'I need to see him about that broken fence. I'll walk over.' A few minutes later, Tom arrived in Charlie's yard. He spotted Charlie and they met up. 'Our lass here?' Charlie shook his head.
'Not seen her today.'
'But she was going to ask you to drive her over to see my dad,' Tom explained.
'Well, she never turned up here. She's not at home, then?' Tom looked puzzled and shook his head. 'Do you want me to run you over to your dad's? I've got time,' offered Charlie.
'Aye, please,' said Tom. 'I can't think where else she might be, but how did she get there, I wonder?'

A little later and they were pulling up in the farmyard. Gertie came out.
'Now, lads.'
'Our Mary here?' asked Tom.
'Never seen her but I've been out in fields. I'll ask dad.' They walked into the house. Dad looked up as the group walked in. 'It's our Tom, Dad, with Charlie, looking for Mary. Have you seen her?' Dad nodded.
'Aye. She came with young Jacob and a Jack Nether...
something,' he replied, standing up. He'd done a lot of thinking after Mary and Jack left. Tom cursed. 'Don't cuss, son. There's things you don't know, things I should have told you about, a long time ago.'
'Dad, you don't know him. He's a nasty piece of work. I don't want my Missus near him.' Dad shook his head.
'He won't hurt Mary, Tom,' he said, emphatically.
'Dad, I'll have to go,' Tom said, and turning to Charlie, asked, 'Will you take me to Jack Netherfield's? Mary must be there.' Charlie nodded.
'I'm coming too,' Dad declared, surprising them all.
'What do you want to come for?' asked Tom. 'He's nothing to do with you, Dad.'

'I know him, Tom,' he insisted, 'and I have a letter for him and some unfinished business to put right.'

He went over to a worn bureau and taking a small key from his pocket, opened a drawer. He shuffled through some papers and brought out an old, faded, tattered envelope.
'What on earth's that?' questioned Gertie. 'Dad, what do you want with this fellow, Jack? You don't know him,' she said, adamantly.
'I tell you, I do,' insisted her dad, raising his voice. 'I'm going with Tom. Charlie will bring me back, won't you, lad?' he asked, turning to Charlie, who, like the others, was very confused. Charlie nodded. Dad took his heavy coat down from behind the door and put it on. He slowly walked out to the van.
'How come you know Jack, Dad?' Tom questioned, walking beside him.
'All in good time, son. All in good time,' was the only reply.
Dad's heart was racing with anticipation of what was to come.
'I'll get in back, Charlie,' said Tom. 'Dad can sit in front.' They set off at speed. Tom was very anxious about Mary.

Back at Jack's place, Mary was getting desperate to leave.
'I won't hurt you, Mary,' said Jack, removing his hands from her face. 'Just say you'll stay, please?' he begged, kissing each of her cheeks. The door opened and in walked Tom, followed by his dad and Charlie.
'Daddy,' shouted Jacob, struggling out of Mary's hold and toddling across the stone floor into Tom's arms. Mary stood up. Jack staggered and sat down, trying to focus on the new arrivals. He gazed at Dad.
'Well, Dad,' he said. 'Come to visit me after all these years, have you?' Mary gasped. Charlie's mouth dropped open, but no words came out. Tom, his body tense and looking at Jack, said,
'Dad? You're talking crazy. You're nothing but a drunk.' Dad took Tom's arm.
'Steady, son. Calm down. As I said before, there's things I need to say, things none of you know.' All eyes turned to him. 'I'll sit down if I may,' he said, politely, lowering himself onto the hard, wooden chair, vacated by Mary.

Looking to Jack, Dad began to talk, hesitantly, struggling to get his words out.

'I'm sorry, Jack. I did write to your mam years ago. See here.' He pulled the faded letter out of his pocket. 'I wrote this and sent it to your mam. I put a letter in for you but your mam had gone and letter came back.' His eyes were filling with tears. Mary reached out and put her arm around his shoulders. He continued, looking over to Tom. 'You see, Tom, I met Josie, a bonny, town lass, bit like your Mary. I fell for her, hook, line and sinker, I did. She was a belter. Then she tells me she's expecting my bairn. Shortly afterwards, Missus tells me she's expecting. I couldn't handle it.' His gaze shifted to Jack. 'I told your mam, Jack, to clear off. I never saw her again. But it cut me t' quick, it did. It was years later that I sent letter, but as I say, it came back. Here, read it.' He passed the letter across the table to Jack as tears rolled down his cheeks.

Jack opened the letter. He found it difficult, focusing, but little by little, he made out the words. He took his time reading it before crumpling it up in his hand. He put his head on the table and cried. Everyone was silent, stunned by this revelation. When Jack calmed down, he began talking.
'I was the eldest lad, you see, Tom, but I got nothing.' The words stumbled out in stops and starts. 'I took my step-dad's name to please my mam. He died before she did. I didn't find out who my real dad was until my mam was dying, some years ago. I'd been given to believe that he'd drowned before I was born. When I learnt the truth and after mam died, I came up here to be near my dad but I didn't have the courage to face him.' He stopped, momentarily, trying to compose himself, before continuing. 'My lass walked out on me, not long after we married, expecting, she was. Thought it was mine and grieved. Later, I found out it was someone else's. You turned up, Tom. I hated seeing you with Mary and your bairns. I wanted what you had and I'd missed out. I wanted revenge.' He raised his head and took another mouthful of whisky. His dad reached out and held his hand. Jack continued. 'I poisoned your colt, Tom. I drowned that sheep. I wanted to get back at you because I envied you. I even befriended your Missus to get back at you but I fell in love with her. You had Dad. You had Mary. You had your bairns. You're a damn lucky bloke. I have nothing.' His head went down and he sobbed uncontrollably.

Tom was numb. So, this is what it was all about. He couldn't take it in. He was speechless. But it was getting on and he knew the children would be home from school shortly. He needed to get back home and he wanted time to clear his head and think. Jack's sobs subsided. Dad stood up. He moved closer to Jack and put his arms around him.

'I'm truly sorry, son,' he said. 'Forgive me?' Jack had waited all these years to hear himself be called *son* by his real dad. He was unable to speak. He felt choked. He made a nodding movement with his head and squeezed his dad's hand. 'Take me home, Charlie,' said Dad, wearily. They walked out, the younger man followed by the older one, who finally, had made his peace.

'Tom, we need to go,' said Mary. She took Jacob from Tom's arms and went over to Jack and patted his back as he rested his head on the table. 'We'll be back,' she said. She made for the door. Tom went over to his brother. He didn't know what to say. He put his hand on Jack's shoulder for a minute. Jack didn't move. Tom went out.

Mary and Tom were still on the cobbles when the shot rang out. Tom turned and ran back inside. Jack was on the floor, a gun beside him and blood oozing from his shoulder. Tom knelt beside him. The brothers gazed at each other.

'Oh, Jack, you didn't need to do this,' Tom stated, gazing into Jack's blue eyes. Mary, having immediately handed Jacob to Tom's dad who was sitting in Charlie's van, rushed back into the farmhouse with Charlie on her heels. She quickly found a towel in the bathroom and with Charlie's help, tied it tightly around Jack's shoulder as best she could to stem the bleeding.

'Couldn't even do a good job of this,' mumbled Jack. 'Too much whisky.'

'I wish I'd known sooner about everything, Jack,' Tom said, gently. 'I always wanted a brother.' Jack's face broke into a slow smile.

'Have my van, Tom,' he whispered, hoarsely. 'Use it for Mary and your bairns.' Tom couldn't speak. Tears blinded his eyes. Jack's eyes slowly closed.

'Jack, hang on. You're not giving up now. We'll get you t' hospital,' said Tom, desperately trying to keep Jack alert.

'Charlie, will you take him t' hospital, fast?' Tom asked. 'I'll take my dad home in Jack's van.' At this, Tom's voice almost broke. It took a moment or two for him to compose himself. 'Mary, you walk over fields and see t' bairns,' he added. 'I'll take Jacob with me. I'll call in at Jack's farm-hand and tell him that Jack's had an accident. I know where he lives. It's not far. He'll look after Jack's farm for him.'

'Aye, I'll take your dad,' said Charlie, 'and,' he added, 'Mary, can you send one of your bairns over to Dorothy to tell her I'll be a bit longer.' Mary nodded.

Days later, Tom and Mary learnt that Jack, although having lost a fair amount of blood, was pulling through. Tom, when visiting his dad with this good news, suggested that Jack, on being discharged from hospital, went to live there for a while to help with his recovery.

'I think he'll like that, Dad,' Tom said, 'and it'll give you both a chance to catch up a bit.' His dad nodded, still coming to terms with all that had happened.

'All family together. How about that,' he said, soberly.

Mary and Tom discussed the events for days, seeing all the past occasions with Jack in a new light.

'So much makes sense now,' Mary volunteered, after another chat with Tom about it. 'Don't you think, Tom?' They were standing outside looking over the pasture, enjoying a woodbine on a rather balmy evening in late September. Tom nodded, still going over in his mind at times, the encounters and words that had taken place between him and Jack.

'Takes some getting used to,' he finally acknowledged, 'but we'll get there. I've been thinking also, Mary, that I know we've had our ups and downs but we've come a long way since arriving here almost nine years ago. It'll soon be winter again. You are happy here, lass, aren't you?' he questioned, putting his arm around her. Mary turned to him and smiled.

'You know that old proverb, Tom. *The grass is greener on the other side of the hill*. Well it certainly wasn't greener for me, not at first, you know. It was a total let down. My dreams were blown away.' She laughed. 'But I've grown to love it here. I wouldn't swop my life for anything, Tom, and it's a grand place to bring up bairns. Who knows, maybe we'll have another,' she added, hugging him close. Stubbing out their cigarettes, they wandered back inside, hand in hand.